A guide to the magical places
of England, Wales & Scotland

By the same author

The hidden world of Scotland Yard
(Hutchinson 1971)

The black treasures of Scotland Yard
(Hamish Hamilton 1973)

London in the country: the growth of Suburbia
(Hamish Hamilton 1975)

The age of agony: the art of healing c 1700–1800
(Constable 1975)

The Royal Parks of London
(Constable 1978)

London Walks
(Constable 1981)

The age of miracles: medicine and surgery in the nineteenth century
(Constable 1981)

Guy Williams

A guide to
The magical places of
England, Wales & Scotland

Constable London

First published in Great Britain 1987
by Constable and Company Limited
10 Orange Street London WC2H 7EG
Copyright © 1987 by Guy Williams
Photoset in Linotron Palatino 9 pt by
Rowland Phototypesetting Ltd
Bury St Edmunds, Suffolk
Printed in Great Britain by
The Bath Press, Avon

British Library CIP data

Williams, Guy
A guide to the magical places of England,
Wales and Scotland.
1. Great Britain – Description and travel
– 1971- – Guide-books
I. Title
914.1'04858   DA650

ISBN 0 09 464490 X

For RICHARD BALKWILL
who is in constant quest for Magical Places

Contents

Illustrations

Introduction

Two thousand years ago, the land that we now call 'Britain' was swampy and thickly wooded. In many places, the thickets were impenetrable. Long distance travellers had to keep to the Ridgeways that ran along the highest ground. There, they were near to some of their Gods. Those Gods shone, and, when they were angry, thundered.

Other Gods lived in 'Annwfn' – the Otherworld or Underworld. Lakes and wells had guardian spirits. Springs were givers of life and health. Rocks and boulders could do amazing things. The sun, moving slowly lower and lower in the sky, had to be placated and persuaded to return, after midwinter, to its rightful place on high from where it could provide, once again, warmth and the means of life. Hunters had to ensure success in the chase by performing strange dances in which men dressed as beasts were, in mime, caught and slaughtered. Magic, in a word, was everywhere. Humans were trying to influence the course of events and to produce marvellous physical phenomena by persuading invisible spiritual beings to intervene. The arts – or pretended arts – of sorcery and witchcraft were in their prime.

Nobody moving round Britain in the last decades of the Twentieth Century could fail to be impressed by the surviving traces of our magical past. Ancient rituals are performed by volunteers in quiet provincial towns, though the origins of those rites are almost entirely forgotten. Inexplicable superstitions linger, and are dutifully observed by people whose grandchildren may well travel, through exact science, to the Moon. Modern life is given an extra dimension if its residual magical elements are examined, and appreciated. This book attempts to chart the possible starting places of such a search.

In every county, shire, region and relevant island, I have asked for the help and advice of the appropriate authority on the spot – in most cases, the Chief Local History Librarian. In all but three instances, aid has been given plentifully and with the utmost good will, and those kind people whose names and addresses are quoted under the heading *Further information from* will know from this how greatly their help has been appreciated.

At the end of each section of this Guide, books are suggested that will provide more detailed information relevant, in the main, to that section and to that section only. In most instances, preference has been given to books published fairly recently that may possibly be still in print, or, if not, are likely to be available from public libraries. In some cases, where they are essential reading for extra-serious students, older works are recommended, and these may usually be consulted in reference libraries or in local history collections. Those seeking the most authoritative sources of the strange tales recounted in this Guide will find them in one or more of these books, that have been locally prescribed.

At the back of the Guide, other works are listed. These have a wider geographical range. The authors, compilers and editors of these have contributed significantly to our fund of magical knowledge. So, too, have the many old countryfolk who, in remote pubs late at night, have muttered to the author of the ghosts, goblins and other supernatural beings known to exist in the vicinity. This Guide is, truly, a magical mix.

GUY WILLIAMS

Dates traditionally given for ancient festivals and ceremonies are apt to be misleading. In many cases, the adoption of the Gregorian Calendar in Britain in 1752 has to be taken into account.

England

Avon

Banwell Hill On this hill, there is a prehistoric earthwork
known as 'The Camp'. In this, there is a big cross, lying flat, but
raised some two feet above the surrounding turf. Local Christians
originally set an upright cross here, it is said, but the Devil kept
sending high winds to blow it down. At last, the locals accepted
the situation.

Bath The healing wells of the old Roman city are said to have
been discovered by a Prince Bladud, son of a king of Ancient
Britain named Lud Hudibras. When he caught leprosy, Bladud
was driven from his father's court, and became a swineherd.
Soon, Bladud's pigs had also contracted the disease. Crazed
by their sufferings, the beasts ran away and dashed into a
foul-smelling marsh. When Bladud got them out, he found that
they were cured, so he used the muddy waters of the marsh to
cure his own leprosy. Freed from the disease, he was welcomed
back at court.

Bleadon Site of a landing-place at which, in the seventh century,
raiding Danish pirates were massacred by the local people.

Bristol Channel Enchanted islands are said to appear and
disappear unpredictably in the estuary of the Severn and in the
Bristol Channel. The immortal inhabitants of the islands are
believed to do their shopping in Laugharne, on the coast of
Dyfed.

Chew Stoke The church, now 'St Andrew's', was formerly
dedicated to St Wigefort, the original 'bearded lady', who, if
appealed to, could be relied on to grant an easy death, or to
dispose of an unwanted husband.

Keynsham Named after Keyne, a sixth-century princess with
healing powers. When she came to this spot, the local lord
gave her some land that was overrun by poisonous snakes.

Undeterred, Keyne turned the snakes into stone. The fossilised ammonites found plentifully in the locality are believed to have resulted from the good works of St Keyne.

Norton Malreward The hilltop camp is said to have been established by a giant called Gorm.

Stanton Drew Megalithic stones here are said to have been wedding guests who rashly went on dancing into the small hours of the Sabbath and for that were (literally) petrified. The stones are reputed to be impossible to count with accuracy.

Stoney Littleton Traditionally, a haunt of fairies.

Further reading
Bailey, John, *Somerset and Avon Ghosts, Witches and Legends,* Redcliffe Press, Bristol, 1985.
Bird, M., *Avon and Somerset Ghosts,* James Pike Ltd, St Ives, Cornwall, 1977.
Sigmund, E., *Avon and Somerset Witchcraft,* James Pike Ltd, St Ives, Cornwall, 1977.

Further information from
The County Reference Librarian, Central Library, College Green, Bristol, BS1 5TL.

Bedfordshire

Bedford The county town, associated with the imprisonment of John Bunyan (1628–88), author of *The Pilgrim's Progress,* and with the Panacea Society, custodians of the mysterious box bequeathed to the world by the prophetess Joanna Southcott (1750–1814). Under the terms of the prophetess's will, the box can only be opened if twenty-four bishops are gathered together to watch. When that happens, writings will be found in the box which will cause war, crime and the other evils of humanity to diminish and, hopefully, even to vanish altogether.

Clophill The ruined church of St Mary on Dead Man's Hill was allegedly used in the 1960s and early 1970s for Black Mass rituals. Attempts are said to have been made to call up the spirits of the dead and to communicate with them.

Icknield Way One of the chief routes of prehistoric England, the Way runs from East Anglia through the Chiltern Hills to Stonehenge.

Keysoe A monument on the west side of the church tower records how on 17 April 1718 one William Dickins fell 132 feet from the steeple to the ground and miraculously came to no harm.

Luton Galley Hill, or 'Gallows Hill', may have been a place of execution and may have been used as a burial place for witches.

Oakley Here, in the eighteenth century, an old woman accused of being a witch was subjected to the traditional trial by ordeal. She was found not guilty and discharged.

Odell A local baron, whose memorial is in the church, is said to have sold his soul to the Devil. When the time came for the Devil to collect, his quarry took refuge in the church. Scratch marks said to have been made in the fabric of the porch by the frustrated claimant are still visible. The baron, it is said, returns in ghostly form, riding a big black charger, once every hundred years.

Stevington Known to John Bunyan, the holy well here may have suggested to the writer the sepulchre into which vanished the load borne by his hero Christian.

Further reading
Brittain, Vera, *In the Steps of John Bunyan*, Rich & Cowan, 1950.
Hurst, George, *Rural Legends*, Provost and Company, 1878.

Further information from
The Principal Assistant Librarian, County Library, County Hall,
    Bedford, MK42 9AP.

Berkshire

Abingdon Morris dancing has taken place here for many years,
usually at times of festivals and fairs.

Aldworth The parish church was once the private chapel of the
Norman de la Beche family. Nine monuments inside the church
commemorate male members of the family, some of whom
appear to have been exceptionally tall. A tenth monument –
dedicated to one 'John Everafraid' – once lay half in and half out
of the church, but has now disappeared. The local tradition is that
John Everafraid bartered his soul with the Devil, in exchange for
worldly treasure. The Devil swore that when the time came he
would get Everafraid's soul, whether he were buried inside the
church or outside. Everafraid arranged, therefore, for his body to
lie partly in, and partly out of, the chuch, hoping in that way to
cheat the Devil of his due.

Bisham The Abbey is said to have been haunted by the ghost of
a Dame Elizabeth Hoby, friend of Queen Elizabeth I. The Dame
died in an unhappy state in 1609, having earlier, by her harsh
treatment of him, caused the death of her insufficiently studious
son.

Hungerford The annual 'Hocktide Festival', observed in the
town shortly after Easter, may or may not have any magical
significance. It is said to have been instituted in 1364 in honour of
John of Gaunt, patron of the town.

Kingston Lisle In the garden of a small house near here there is
a large boulder or 'Blowing Stone'. From this, it is said, King
Alfred managed to send trumpet-like calls that roused his loyal
forces and brought them into action against the hated invaders.

Newbury The town and its surrounding parishes have been, for
centuries, renowned for the witches who have lived here and
practised their arts in spite of much local opposition. Particularly
frequented by the witches has been Cottington's Hill, one mile or
so south of Kingsclere.

   According to a seventeenth-century pamphlet, one of the local
witches was seen by some of Cromwell's soldiers standing on a
small plank board and sailing on it over the river of Newbury (the
Kennet). When the soldiers tried to shoot her, the witch caught
their bullets in her hands. Then, with derisive laughter, she
put the bullets in her mouth and chewed them. She was
overpowered by one of the soldiers who slashed her forehead –
a most effective way of dealing with witches, it was believed.
Having her at his mercy, the soldier then 'discharged a pistol
underneath her ear, at which she straight sank down and died'.

Uffington Until recently in Berkshire, the Uffington White Horse
and the empty Stone Age burial chamber known as 'Wayland's
Smithy' are included here under Oxfordshire.

Windsor The Castle is said to be haunted by several royal ghosts
– Elizabeth I has been heard walking through the Library and
Henry VIII through the Cloisters; George III looks out through a
window at soldiers on the parade ground, as he used to do when
he was mentally ill and kept in confinement at Windsor; and
there are others, less specifically identified.

   For many centuries, the Great Park has been associated with

the ghost of Herne the Hunter, mentioned by William
Shakespeare in *The Merry Wives of Windsor*:

> . . . There is an old tale goes that Herne the hunter,
> Sometime a keeper here in Windsor Forest,
> Doth all the winter-time, at still midnight,
> Walk round about an oak, with great ragg'd horns . . .

The identity of Herne has been hotly debated. Some say that he
was a royal huntsman who committed some offence and then,
convinced that he would be disgraced and, at least, dismissed
from the royal service, hanged himself from the oak tree he was
afterwards to haunt. Other authorities claim that he was gravely
injured by a wounded stag that was charging at his royal master.
Herne was then resuscitated by a wizard who told the king to cut
off the stag's antlers and tie them to the huntsman's head. For
some time after that, the restored Herne basked in his master's
favour, but this made the other huntsmen envious, and
eventually they persuaded the king to dismiss him, driving the
man, again, to suicide by hanging. Modern scholarship suggests
that the horned figure's association with the park and an oak tree
is much older than any royal connection with Windsor and that
Herne is, in fact, Cernunnos, the Celtic god of the underworld,
focal figure of a pre-Christian cult. Whatever his origins may be,
Herne is popularly supposed to appear, warning-wise, before
each outstanding national disaster.

Further reading
Berkshire Federation of Women's Institutes, *The New Berkshire
    Village Book*, Countryside Books, 1985.
Millson, Cecilia, *Tales of Old Berkshire*, Countryside Books, 1977.

Further information from
The Principal Librarian, Local Studies, Central Library, Abbey
    Square, Reading, RG1 3BQ.

Buckinghamshire

Colnbrook   The Ostrich Inn stands on a site used for such taverns since the twelfth century. For a time, in the Middle Ages, the inn was kept by a couple named Jarman who murdered their wealthier guests by dropping them through a trapdoor into a vat of boiling ale. Their perfidy was discovered when the horse of one of their victims – Thomas Cole, a rich clothier – was found wandering loose, which started a search for Cole. The Jarmans were hanged in Windsor Forest.

Great Kimble   Near a public footpath that runs through Chequers Park there is a small motte-and-bailey earthwork known in the past as 'Cymbeline's Mount' but now more often referred to as 'Cymbeline's Castle'. This may or may not have some connection with the British king Cunobelin (died about AD 43). Equally suspect is the local tradition that anyone running seven times round the earthwork will see the Devil.

Medmenham   In the mid-eighteenth century Sir Francis Dashwood, owner of West Wycombe Park, presided over a private society known as 'The Knights of St Francis'. Membership of this secret association was limited strictly to twenty-four men, and those invited to join had to be of an agreeably high social standing. During the summer months the members met at Medmenham Abbey, where they were popularly supposed to hold Black Masses and other mysterious rituals. Before long, Sir Francis's association had become more generally known as 'The Hellfire Club', and the caves excavated for the members and their magic practices in a hillside at West Wycombe are still called 'The Hellfire Caves', though the club ceased to function after 1763.

North Marston   In 1290 a Master John Schorne, once sub-deacon of Monks Risborough, became rector of North Marston. Three years later, in a time of serious drought, he struck his staff against the baked, cracked earth, and immediately a spring of cold, drinkable water welled upwards. The waters so miraculously called up quickly became known throughout southern England and the Midlands for their healing properties and they were especially valued by sufferers from the ague. At one time, John Schorne's Well was the third most important place of pilgrimage in England.

Schorne was also noted for another considerable achievement – he is reputed to have captured the Devil and to have kept him prisoner in a boot. The deed came to be commemorated in church glass, in paintings and carvings, and on rood screens, some of them as far away as East Anglia, where ague was almost endemic. Usually Satan, ringed and horned, is shown peeping out of a boot that is nearly half as tall as John Schorne himself. Schorne, in hood and gown, holds with one hand the boot and its wrinkled occupant while, with the other hand, he makes a sign of blessing.

Olney   The pancake race held at Olney on Shrove Tuesday has, in recent years, attracted international attention, but it is unlikely that it has much, if any, magical significance. One theory is that the race originated in 1445, when a housewife making pancakes heard the bell calling the villagers to church and ran there, taking her pan with her.

Wendover   Described by R. L. Stevenson as a 'straggling, purposeless sort of place', Wendover has a church said to be built on a site chosen for it by witches or fairies. The authorities wanted the church to be in a more accessible position, but the materials were carried to the present site by unseen hands.

West Wycombe   See **Medmenham**, above.

Wingrave   During the late eighteenth century an inoffensive old Wingrave woman named Susanna Hannokes was accused by one of her neighbours of witchcraft – Susanna had put a spell on her spinning-wheel, the neighbour said, so that its owner could not make it go round. After being hailed by her accuser and the accuser's husband before a magistrate, Susanna was taken to Wingrave Church, stripped of her clothes and weighed on a pair of scales against the church Bible. To the great mortification of her accusers, she passed the ordeal triumphantly, outweighing the Bible, and was thereupon acquitted of the charge against her.

Winslow A public house here is called 'The Devil in the Boot', commemorating the achievement of John Schorne of North Marston (q.v.). Several 'Boot Inns' in various parts of southern England may once have sheltered pilgrims going to or from Schorne's Well.

Further reading
Cull & Ogan, *Picture of Buckinghamshire*, Robert Hale, 1985.

Further information from
The Senior Assistant County Librarian (Reference and Information), County Library, County Hall, Aylesbury, Buckinghamshire, HP20 1UU.

Cambridgeshire and the Fens

Cambridge The quiet rooms and passages of Cambridge's ancient colleges are reputedly haunted by a number of ghosts. In Corpus Christi the shade of Doctor Butts, Master of the College from 1626 to 1632, is said to appear in the rooms in which he committed suicide on Easter Sunday in the latter year. In Merton Hall, a big, fur-covered animal or bird is said to loom from the darkness from time to time. In St John's, another Master – Doctor Wood, who died in 1839 – is said to return, in attenuated form, to the staircase on which, as an impoverished undergraduate, he used to study, relying on the college's candle because he was unable to afford one of his own. Abbey House, on the Newmarket Road, built on the site of an Augustinian priory, has a 'Grey Lady', and the fur-covered beast of Merton Hall has also appeared here.

Ely A ghostly barge is said to pass mysteriously, on some misty evenings, along the Little Ouse towards the city. On the barge are the ghosts of a number of monks who have with them an open coffin containing a female corpse. This corpse is presumed to be that of St Withburga, who was buried at East Dereham, Norfolk (q.v.) in the year 654. More than three centuries later, the then Abbot of Ely arranged for the saint's body to be forcibly exhumed and transferred to Ely. There, he believed, it would draw pilgrims, and, with them, much badly-needed money. His scheme went wrong when the saint's empty grave in Norfolk filled up with water, and this proved to have miraculous healing qualities. The pilgrims, after that, preferred to take their cash to East Dereham.

Haddenham Here, in 1647, a woman called Thomason Read was tried for witchcraft. She had claimed that the Devil had appeared to her in the form of a large mouse and had repeatedly drawn blood from her body. Unusually for those accused of witchcraft at the time, she was acquitted.

Heydon The ancient defensive earthwork known as 'Heydon Ditch' is said to be haunted by the ghosts of exceptionally tall Saxons, slain here in the past. Headless semi-giant skeletons have been unearthed here by archaeologists.

Horseheath Money Lane, here, is said to be haunted by the ghost of a former villager who once hid some treasure in the lane and, since his death, returns from time to time to look for it.

Witches were active in and around Horseheath at least until the early years of the twentieth century. One of the most notorious of these powerful females – an ancient bony creature, half-clothed in rags – was known as 'Daddy Witch'. She claimed that she had gained most of her mystical knowledge from a book called *The Devil's Plantation*. When Daddy Witch died in 1860, her body was buried in the middle of the road which leads from Horseheath to

Horseheath Green. Her grave was said to remain dry, even in rainy weather, owing to the heat of her body. Horseheath folk used to nod nine times before passing over her grave, in order to avoid bad luck.

Leverington   Until the end of the nineteenth century, Mid-Lent Sunday was marked in Leverington by a festival, with games and sports. Small cakes known as 'Whirling Cakes' were specially baked for consumption at the festivities. They were given their name, it was said, in memory of an old woman of Leverington who, the story went, was making cakes for some visitors on one Feast Sunday when the Devil appeared before her in a whirlwind and carried her off over the church steeple.

Littleport   Old Mrs Gooby, of Littleport, and Granny Gray, who died there in 1898, were famous for their semi-magical 'cures'. The ingredients in their reputedly effective poultices were, principally, such rudimentary substances as fresh cow dung, mare's milk, and the last urine passed by a person about to die.

   Some Littleport girls, traditionally, have pinned great faith in yarrow (*Achillea millefolium*) as a love herb. Others have worn fur tippets in which they have inserted small silk sachets containing snippets of their own and their future husbands' pubic hair, believing that this would guarantee a happy married life.

Long Stanton   This place was the home of two notorious and mysterious females: the 'whimsical woman' Margaret Pryor, who went to Court in 1659 saying that a company of Quakers had turned her into a horse and had ridden her to a banquet four miles away; and Bet Cross, the village witch of the late nineteenth century, who was said to fly round the district on a hurdle, and to be able, by magic, to efface the memory of her feats from the mind of anyone who saw her.

Peterborough   The arrival of Henry of Poitou, appointed as Abbot of Peterborough in 1127 simply because he was a relation of Henry II, was followed by the appearance in the district of a pack of 'black and wide-eyed and loathsome' hounds, hunted by some equally repellent and equally ghostly men, mounted on black horses and black goats. The new abbot proved to be greedy and of no benefit to the neighbourhood. The ominous pack of spectral hounds has reappeared at intervals, it is said, until quite recently, foretelling each time some death or disaster.

Reach The Devil's Dyke – the great earthwork raised, probably, in the fifth or sixth century – runs from Reach along a seven-mile course as far as Wood Ditton. It is said locally to have been thrown up by Satan, or, alternatively, by giants. There is another saying repeated often in the district: 'If you walk round Reach Church seven times the Devil will appear'.

Sawston Sawston Hall, built by Mary Tudor to reward the Catholic Huddleston family for their loyalty to her, is reputed often to have been revisited by the shade of that unhappy Queen – perhaps because at Sawston she had for once found peace of mind.

Wandlebury This Iron Age fort on the summit of the Gog Magog Hills was once a stronghold of the Iceni, and, later, a Roman military encampment. Many tales are told of this bleak place. The oldest is that included by Gervase of Tilbury in his *Otia Imperialia*, written about the year 1211:

> On the hilltop, there is a level space surrounded with entrenchments and with a single entrance, like a gate. There is a very ancient tradition, attested by popular report, that if a warrior enters this level space at the dead of night, when the moon is shining, and cries 'Knight to knight, come forth', immediately he will be confronted by a warrior, armed for fight, who charging horse to horse, either dismounts his adversary or is dismounted. But I should state that the warrior must enter the enclosure alone, although his companions may look on from outside . . .

According to Gervase, a Norman knight called Osbert decided to test the truth of this story and managed to defeat the ghostly warrior. He took his adversary's fierce black horse back to Cambridge with him. At cockcrow next morning, however, the horse 'prancing, snorting and pawing the earth, suddenly burst the reins that held it and regained its native liberty'. It was never seen again.

West Wratting   The countryside near here is said to have been haunted by a jet-black, shaggy-haired creature known as 'The Shug Monkey'.

Whittlesford   It was long believed, here, that on St Mark's Eve (25 April) the apparitions of those destined to die within the next twelve months would enter the churchyard at midnight to inspect the places chosen for their graves. Those about to marry were also said by some to have a part in this ghostly ritual.

Wisbech   An old woman named Mrs Reeve of Lake's End, near Wisbech, was credited, towards the end of the nineteenth century, with supernatural powers. As late as 1936, an old man who had offended her in his youth remembered how she had bewitched him, so that he became covered with lice.

Wisbech, home of the legendary giant 'Tom Hickathrift', is also associated with 'Toadmen': men who, in the past, would catch a live toad and would then either skin it and de-flesh it or would peg it to an ant-heap until the ants had eaten the bones clean. One of the toad's bones was believed to give the man who carried it some magical power over horses.

Further reading
Porter, Enid, *Cambridgeshire Customs and Folklore*, Routledge & Kegan Paul Ltd, 1969.

Further information from
The Local Studies Librarian, Central Library, 7 Lion Yard, Cambridge, CB2 3QD.

Cheshire

Alderley Edge   A natural spring on this sandstone cliff or 'edge' is said to be a wishing well, and locals say that the water falls 'by the wizard's will'. The wizard referred to is Merlin, who, according to the legend, once opened a pair of huge gates in a nearby rock and showed a local farmer the cave in which King Arthur and his knights are sleeping, waiting for the day when England will need them again.

Alvanley   People leap through flames here, in spring and autumn: this habit is believed to have survived from Celtic seasonal rituals.

Antrobus   Here – and at Comberbach, Frodsham, Halton, Malpas, Tarporley and possibly some other small Cheshire towns – groups of young people have customarily sung and danced on All Souls' Day, receiving for their trouble small spiced 'soul cakes', or, nowadays, money. This undertaking is supposed to remind all observers of the inevitability of death, while celebrating, at the same time, the continuity of human existence.

Appleton   A thorn tree here is said to have been grown from a cutting taken from the famous tree at Glastonbury in Somerset (q.v.). At the ceremony of 'bawming the thorn', held in high summer, the tree was decorated with flowers and ribbons.

Bramhall   On New Year's Eve, 1630, a rider in red stayed overnight at Bramhall Hall. On the following morning, the owner of the Hall, William Davenport, was found dead. The red rider had disappeared, but he is said to return every year on New Year's Eve.

Bramhall Hall

Bunbury A cottage on the Whitchurch road is decorated with stone figures and faces. These are said to have been carved by a poacher on his return from transportation, and they represent those responsible for his capture and punishment, whom he wished to curse.

Capesthorne A severed hand is said to have been seen tapping on a window of Capesthorne Hall, in 1958, by William Bromley-Davenport.

Chester The George and Dragon Inn stands on the site of a Roman cemetery. The steady steps of a Roman legionary – presumably still on sentry duty – have been said to have been heard on the inn's upper floor.

Church Coppenhall Home, during the early eighteenth century, of the famous 'white' witch Bridget Bostock. Many people travelled long distances to see her, believing that by her 'fasting spittle' and the application of her hand she could cure them of their ailments.

Combermere The ghost of a little girl is said to have haunted Combermere Abbey, foretelling by her appearance the death of some member of the family that occupied the place.

 The mere, too, has associations with the supernatural – it is one of several British lakes into which a church bell has accidentally fallen, or has been dragged by unseen hands. In this case, the man ferrying the bell over the mere is said to have cursed, whereupon he, too, promptly disappeared.

Congleton The Neolithic chambered tomb known as 'The Bridestones' is said locally to have an atmosphere of mystery.

Delamere Forest A pamphlet dated AD 1600 tells of a remarkably effective healing well here, to be found at the base of a holly tree.

Disley In Lyme Park, a ghostly funeral procession is said to appear from time to time. Presumably, it is that of the second Sir Piers Legh, who died of his wounds shortly after fighting at Agincourt. The weeping white-robed figure who follows the procession is said to be Sir Piers's lover Blanche, who died broken-hearted after she lost her man. A similar figure has been seen inside Lyme Hall.

Farndon Cries of children have been heard unexpectedly at night beneath the bridge here. The cries are believed to recall those of the two sons of the Welsh prince Madoc, who were murdered on the spot in the early fourteenth century.

Marbury Marbury Hall – ancient, but largely rebuilt in the 1840s in the French style – was said to be haunted by a mysterious White Lady: connected, possibly, with an embalmed body once kept in the house.

Marple The River Goyt, here, is said to be haunted by a girl whose Royalist lover was drowned in its waters.

Neston A ghostly priest is said to have appeared at the Catholic church here, and to have taken a service.

Over The old parish church – originally, it is believed, in the middle of the town – is said to have been carried away from there by the Devil. Startled by the ringing of the bells at Vale Royal Abbey, he dropped the church on its present site.

In the fifteenth century, Over was the home of the rustic prophet Robert Nixon, who predicted successfully the Battle of Bosworth Field and other events. More questionably, he foresaw that foreign nations would invade England 'with snow on their helmets'.

Plumley At Tabley Old Hall, two ghostly figures have been seen on a balcony, or so it is said. The male shade is that of a guest, once killed here in a duel. The female figure is his wife, the cause of the duel, who committed suicide after it. Both bodies are believed to have been sealed up in a secret room, to avoid scandal.

Rostherne A mermaid is said to live in (or to visit) the mere. Each Easter Sunday, at dawn, she is believed to sing and to ring an underwater bell that once rolled from the church into the mere.

Weaverham The 'healing well' here has an unusual property – anyone drinking from it is supposed to be certain to return to the village, even if departing for the wars.

Further reading
Hole, Christina, *Traditions and Customs of Cheshire*, Williams & Norgate, 1937.
Rickman, P., *Mysterious Cheshire*, Dalesman, 1980.
Woods, F., *Legends and Traditions of Cheshire*, Shiva, 1982.
Woods, F., *Further Legends and Traditions of Cheshire*, Shiva, 1983.

Further information from
The Local Studies Advisor, Central Library, Museum Street, Warrington, WA1 1JB.

Cleveland

Guisborough For centuries, local people have believed that there is an underground passage connecting the twelfth-century Priory here to the Plantation Field in Tocketts, a little to the north. In this passage, there is said to be a large chest full of gold that is guarded by a fierce crow or raven. Only once has this chest been seen by human eye. That happened when a particularly courageous man managed to find and explore the tunnel. Then, the watchful bird is said to have changed, instantly, into the Devil, who drove the intruder savagely away.

Handale This village near Liverton was once supposedly haunted by a serpent which had an insatiable appetite for virtuous maidens. A local youth eventually killed the monster and managed to rescue the girl it was about to devour.

Marske-by-the-Sea Some centuries ago, the old church here was condemned, and plans were made for building a new church on a different site. Part of the old fabric was demolished, and the stones were carted to the new location. When the workmen returned on the following morning, they were surprised to find the old church whole again. Every stone had been replaced *in situ*, and the mortar which had been used to reset the displaced stones was as hard as that used hundreds of years before. Each night, after that, the work of the rebuilders was similarly frustrated until, realising that they were being opposed by a 'hobman' or supernatural being and his friends, they abandoned the project.

Further information from
The Central Reference Librarian, County Library, Victoria
   Square, Middlesbrough, Cleveland, TS1 2AY.

Cornwall

Altarnun To St Non's Well, here, insane people used to be taken and forcibly ducked in its supposedly healing waters. After prolonged immersion they would be taken to the local church, where mass would be sung.

Bodmin Moor The Moor is said to be haunted by the ghost of the wicked magistrate Jan Tregeagle, who was condemned to endless torment for the sins he had committed during his lifetime. To save him from the clutches of the Devil, the local clergy gave Tregeagle a limpet shell with holes in it and ordered him to empty all the water from the supposedly bottomless Dozmary Pool.

Another ghost associated with the Moor is that of a murdered sailor seen, occasionally, outside the well-known Jamaica Inn.

Boleigh The nineteen stones in the circle here are usually known as 'The Merry Maidens'. Near them are two more stones, 'The Pipers', whose music the maidens were forbidden to hear. Unable to resist the temptation, the girls are said to have danced to the music of the pipes, and to have suffered the inevitable consequence.

Camelford King Arthur is said to have fought his last battle near the River Camel, about a mile above the town.

Carn Brea On the high ground here, between Camborne and Redruth, bonfires have traditionally been kindled at Midsummer, and various customs, almost certainly of pre-Christian origin, have been observed. It is said to be particularly lucky for observers to jump over the glowing embers of one of the ritual fires.

Helston Famed internationally for its annual festival – held, now, on the Saturday nearest to 8 May, the feast of St Michael. The origins of 'Floral Day' or 'Furry Day' are obscure, but the decorations put up in the town and the dancing that enlivens its streets are often said to commemorate the triumph of the saint over the Devil and his fiends, who are supposed to have been particularly troublesome at Helston.

Land's End The entrance to the once-fertile but now submerged land of Lyonesse is said by some to have been, many hundreds of years ago, at Land's End. Certainly, a chair-shaped rock here was the seat of the notorious witch Madgy Figgy. She profited by the ghoulish activities of the local wreckers, who lured ships to their doom.

Launceston Dockacre House here is said to be haunted by the ghost of a woman who, in the early eighteenth century, went mad and was starved to death. The ghost of her husband, who is believed to have been responsible for her sad fate, is said also to appear from time to time. He plays a flute – it is alleged – when a death in the household is imminent.

Liskeard A group of stones near here is known as 'The Hurlers'. The stones are said to have been, previously, men who sinfully played on the Sabbath day the old Cornish sport called 'Hurling'. (See **St Columb Major, Cornwall**, below.)

Looe The water of a well here was believed to bring fertility to the barren. A visit to St Keyne's Well, near the town, traditionally ensured mastery in marriage for the partner who got there first. As Robert Southey observed in a good-humoured ballad:

> . . . I hastened as soon as the wedding was o'er
> And left my good wife in the porch,
> But i' faith she had been wiser than I
> For she took a bottle to church.

Ludgvan The well at Ludgvan contained water that was guaranteed to protect those baptised in it from being hanged. Trencom Hill, near the town, has a small Iron Age fort on its summit. Here, it is said, giants used to live, keeping their treasure for safety inside the hill. A rash villager who thought he knew where the treasure was hidden once went up the hill by moonlight and started to dig. Immediately a mighty storm broke, and the lightning was so bright that the surprised intruder was able to see a crowd of 'spriggans', or violent fairies, emerge from the rocks and move threateningly towards him. He fled in terror, suffering so great a shock that for a long time after he was confined to his bed.

Madron A ring of granite a little more than two miles to the north-west of Madron is called 'Men-an-Tol', or 'Stone-with-a-Hole'. For centuries, it has been used for healing purposes. Scrofulous children are passed naked through it at least three times and then rubbed on the grass, and adults are squeezed through it in attempts to cure rheumatism and other disorders. Another long-famed resort for the sick is Madron Well, where Bishop Hall of Exeter saw, in 1640, a man who had been crippled for sixteen years restored, through the well's waters, to full mobility.

Marhamchurch   A 'revel' is held annually here, on the Monday following 12 August. The festival commemorates the pious St Marwenne, who is supposed to have founded a monastic settlement on the spot, but it is possible that it may have more ancient origins.

Padstow   The Hobby Horse Ceremony held annually at Padstow on May Day is almost certainly based on a pre-Christian fertility rite or sun-respecting observance. The ceremony starts on the previous evening, just before midnight, when singing townspeople move through the darkened streets. On the day itself, two hobby-horses – one old, and one of more recent creation – dance about the town, each being accompanied by a Master of Ceremonies, by musicians, and by a team of 'mayers' dressed in colours appropriate to the 'oss' they support. At intervals the horses, portrayed by masked men in ample black capes, sink to the ground and pretend to die, but are revived and dance again to this cheerful refrain:

> With the merry ring, adieu the merry spring,
>   For summer is a-come unto day,
> How happy is the little bird that merrily does sing,
>   In the merry morning of May.

Penzance   The ghost of an old sea-captain is said to have been seen and heard at the Dolphin Inn. He is thought to have been, in his lifetime, a smuggler – or, perhaps, a victim of Judge Jeffreys, who is believed to have presided over trials in the room of the inn now used for dining.

Polperro   The cave known as 'Willy Willcock's Hole' on the western side of the harbour is believed to be haunted by the ghost of a fisherman who lost his way in the maze-like tunnels to which the entrance leads. The ghost's cries are said to be audible on dark and windy nights.

Rillaton The ghost of a druid is said to have haunted a burial mound near Rillaton Manor. The 'druid' would offer passers-by a golden cup from which to drink. A real gold beaker was found in 1818 during excavations near Rillaton. The beaker is now in the British Museum.

St Austell On the Mengue Stone, set in a pavement here, a witch is said to have been burned to death.

St Columb Major Traditionally a centre for 'hurling', the game played with a wooden ball covered with silver gilt. Some say that the game has ancient origins; that passing the ball from hand to hand brings good luck to those that touch it; and that this is a vestigial reminder of sun worship.

St Ives Here, too, a silver ball is used for 'hurling'. At St Ives, the game is usually played on a Monday in February. At other times of the year, the ghost of a lady with a lantern is seen wandering among the rocks off St Ives. She is searching pathetically for a child she lost when the ship they were on was wrecked nearby – or so it is believed.

St Just This is one of several mining centres in Cornwall where workers underground have been continually aware of the 'knockers' – mysterious small creatures who, if appeased, would guide the miners by their tapping to the richest lodes of tin. If they were annoyed – as, for example, by miners who whistled, or who spied on them – they were quick to bring misfortune to the offender.

St Keyne See **Looe**.

St Michael's Mount According to local legends, the Mount was once the home of a giant called Cormoran who, with his wife Cormelian, built the upper parts out of white rock. Once, when

Cormoran was sleeping, his wife tried to bring some of the local greenstone, which did not have to be carried as far as the granite. When Cormoran woke and found out what had been going on, he kicked his wife so hard that her apron string broke. The greenstone boulder she was carrying tumbled out and rolled down to the causeway, where it can still be seen.

In the buildings on the Mount there is a rocky chair. St Keyne is said to have endowed this seat with the same mysterious properties as the saint's well near Looe (q.v.).

St Neots St Neot is said to have been a dwarf, and was famed for his miraculous achievements with animals, birds and fishes. One of the saint's most remarkable feats, in which he restored two dead fish to life, is recalled in a stained glass window in the church.

St Sampson The Iron Age hill fort known as 'Castle Dore' has been said to have once been the home of King Mark, featured in the sad story of Tristan and Iseult.

Sennen On the Holy Rock, near Sennen, the first of a cross-county chain of bonfires used to be kindled on Midsummer Eve. (See also **Carn Brea**.)

Talland The church here is reputed to have been planned for Pulpit, further inland. Each night, though, the stones used during the day were moved by supernatural means to their present position on Talland Hill.

Tintagel The ruined castle is often said to have been the birthplace of King Arthur, but as it was not built until the twelfth century this is unlikely, to say the least. The cave below the castle is usually called 'Merlin's' by local guides but factual evidence for this, too, is slight. The romantic Victorians loved the place, however tenuous its associations with the legendary past.

Truro Wassailers, deriving their name from the Old English words *waes hael*, meaning 'be of good health', keep up their traditional festivities around Christmas and New Year's Day in several Cornish towns and villages. The Truro Wassailers are particularly well organised, singing outside houses and inns their welcome benediction:

> I hope that your apple-trees will prosper and bear,
> And bring forth good cider when we come next year.

Zennor Cornish witches are said to have met, each Midsummer Eve, at Witches' Rock, near here. Anyone who touched the rock nine times at midnight was believed to be protected afterwards against evil and misfortune. Zennor is also one of the many places in Cornwall favoured by mermaids. The best-known Zennor mermaid is reputed regularly to have attended services, for many years, in Zennor Church. Then she was attracted to, and fell in love with, Matthew Trewhella, son of the churchwarden and possessor of a particularly fine voice. The couple left the village and were never seen there again – they had gone to live beneath the waves, the villagers assumed. A fifteenth-century carved bench-end in Zennor Church shows the fish-tailed lady, equipped with her mirror and comb.

Further reading

Bottrell, William, *Traditions and Hearthside Stories of West Cornwall*, Wm. Bottrell, Penzance, 1870–80.

Courtney, M. A., *Cornish Feasts and Folklore*, Beare, Penzance, 1890.

Deane, Tony, and Shaw, Tony, *The Folklore of Cornwall*, Batsford, 1975.

Further information from

The County Local Studies Library, Redruth Library, Clinton Road, Redruth, TR15 2QE.

Cumbria

Ambleside   Here, and in several other places in Cumbria, rushes are carried with much ceremony into the church at an annual festival. The custom arose through the need to have dry warm coverings for the damp earthen floors of churches and dwellings before these were paved, and is unlikely to have much, if any, magical significance. In earlier centuries, though, Maypole dancing and other primitive junketings followed the strewing of the rushes.

Cross Fell   The rolling moorland here was known as 'Fiends' Fell' until at least 1479, indicating that the early Dalesmen believed that the fierce Helm Wind which comes down from the Pennine summits is due to the activity of demons. The later name suggests that a cross or even a chapel may at one time have been set up on the high ground to counteract the demonic powers.

Derwentwater   An island in this beautiful lake was once the home of the hermit priest St Herbert, who devoted his life to prayer. According to the Venerable Bede, St Herbert and St Cuthbert were close friends and used to meet once a year at Carlisle. In the year 687 St Cuthbert, sensing that his own death was not far away, said that he and St Herbert would probably not meet again in this world. St Herbert then suggested that St Cuthbert should pray that they might be allowed to die simultaneously. Their wishes were granted. Both died at exactly the same hour on 19 March 687.

Eamont Bridge   A cave by the Eamont River was believed to be the home of a giant called 'Isir', who liked eating human flesh. It has also been designated as the probable home of Uther Pendragon, father of King Arthur. Pendragon, too, had cannibalistic tendencies.

Eden Hall   Some time in the Middle Ages, members of the
Musgrave family of Eden Hall obtained a glass beaker with a
flared rim. The beaker, cunningly decorated with coloured
enamels and gilded, was made in Syria and may have been
brought back to England by a warrior returning from the
Crusades. Before long, the beaker became known as 'The Luck of
Eden Hall', and was carefully cherished lest damage to it should
cause some disaster to come to the Musgraves. By 1791, strange
stories had become attached to the beaker. A writer in the
Gentleman's Magazine for August in that year reported:

> Tradition . . . says, that a party of Fairies were drinking and
> making merry round a well near the Hall, called St Cuthbert's
> Well; but, being interrupted by the intrusion of some curious
> people, they were frightened, and made a hasty retreat, and
> left the cup in question: one of the last screaming out,

> If this cup should break or fall,
> Farewell the Luck of Edenhall.

Henry Wadsworth Longfellow, fascinated by this story,
produced in 1834 a translation of a German ballad which
purported to tell how the beaker was inadvertently broken at a
feast, with fatal results:

> In storms the foe with fire and sword;
> He in the night had scaled the wall,
> Slain by the sword lies the youthful Lord,
> But holds in his hand the crystal tall,
> The shattered Luck of Edenhall.

In spite of these gloomy prognostications, the beaker remained
safely in the hands of the Musgrave family until 1926 when they
lent it, with its leather case, to London's Victoria and Albert
Museum. Local people still say that this affected the Musgrave
fortunes, for Eden Hall was demolished eight years later. The
beaker was purchased by the Museum authorities in 1958. St

Cuthbert's Well, mentioned in the *Gentleman's Magazine*, can still be seen near the former site of the mansion.

Egremont   The ruined castle is said to have been occupied in the twelfth century by members of the De Lacy family. In the castle, there hung a great horn which, it was believed, only the rightful lord could blow. While the rightful lord ('Sir Eustace') was away on a Crusade, he was captured and held to ransom. His younger brother ('Sir Hubert') refused to send out the ransom money, and regarded himself from then on as the rightful lord. But Sir Eustace managed to escape, and returned to Egremont. He arrived just as his usurping brother was having a hearty dinner in the castle's Great Hall. The horn at the gate sounded. Sir Hubert, realising that his double-dealing was discovered, departed with urgency.

Grasmere   The rush-bearing procession here attracts much attention. (See **Ambleside**, above.)

Great Corby   Corby Castle is one of several places in England said to be haunted by a 'Radiant Boy' – a shining child that is usually benevolent, but may appear in order to warn some member of the occupying family of imminent disaster.

Kirkby Lonsdale   The Devil's Bridge across the Lune is said to have been built by Satan when he was in a particularly tricky mood. Seeing an old woman whose cow was on the wrong side of the swollen river, he offered to build a bridge for her by the following morning. In return, he told her that he would want the first living thing to cross over the new bridge. The old woman agreed to the bargain. When she returned next morning, the bridge had been built, and the Devil was waiting to collect his due – which, he confidently expected, would be the old woman when she crossed the bridge to retrieve her cow. He was out-tricked, though – she produced a little dog that she had hidden in her cloak, and, throwing a bun to the further side of the river, urged the dog to cross the bridge. The Devil was furious, because he did not want the dog. Having no soul, it would be of no value to him. He rushed off, leaving behind his own neck-collar, which he had temporarily discarded while he was hard at work. (It can still be seen, if one looks downstream, on the right bank between the old bridge and the new. The Devil's fingermarks can be traced, too. He left them on the coping stone of the second recess on the right going towards Casterton.) At several places within easy reach of Kirkby Lonsdale there are stones or boulders said to have been dropped by the Devil in his haste to build the bridge – a pile of stones at Braida Garth, at the head of Kingdale, and a cairn on Casterton Fell being two often-cited examples of Satanic debris.

Levens Several ghosts are said to haunt Levens Hall – a lady in pink has been seen there, and a phantom black dog. Most poignant of the Hall's spectres is, perhaps, the shade of a gipsy woman who, during the eighteenth century, was turned away from the threshold and died shortly after from starvation.

Little Salkeld The great stone circle known as 'Long Meg and her Daughters' was probably assembled in the Bronze Age, possibly for ceremonial purposes, but several alternative theories about the origins of this prehistoric monument have been advanced. According to one story, the thirteenth-century magician Michael Scot found a coven of witches holding their Sabbath here and, enraged, turned them all to stone. Another and more orthodox account explains that Long Meg was a giantess who, with her daughters, was rash enough to dance on a Sunday. A third version refers to the stones as Meg's illicit lovers. It has been said, locally, that if a piece of stone is broken off Long Meg she will bleed. Celia Fiennes, visiting Little Salkeld in the seventeenth century, noted that the local people believed that the Long Meg stones 'cannot be counted twice alike, as is the story of Stonige' (Stonehenge). It was also locally believed that to interfere with the stones would call down supernatural retribution. When a Colonel Lacy tried to shift some of them with explosives, such a storm broke overhead that his workmen ran away in terror.

Mallerstang   The ruins of Pendragon Castle, above the River
Eden, are associated with a mysterious change of name.
Originally the stronghold, built by Hugh de Morville, one of the
murderers of Thomas à Becket, was known as 'Mallerstang
Castle'. Then in 1309 Robert de Clifford, one of Edward I's
greatest supporters, was given a licence to crenellate the place,
which had by then been renamed by him 'Pendragon'. De
Clifford is thought, by this, to have been proclaiming his
assumed descent from Uther Pendragon, father of King Arthur.
To strengthen the castle's defences, de Clifford had a great moat
dug, intending to divert into it the waters of the Eden. 'All to no
purpose', reported Thomas Fuller, author of *The History of the
Worthies of England*, published in 1622. Fuller added, gleefully,
this 'proverb', well known in the district:

> *Let* Uter-Pendragon *do what he can,*
> *The River* Eden *will run as it ran.*

Penrith   Close to St Andrew's Church there are two stone pillars
thought to mark the ends of the grave of Ewan Caesarius, a local
giant who lived and died in the fifth century. They are five yards
apart.

Ravenglass   The Penningtons of Muncaster Castle, near
Ravenglass, were given an enamelled glass bowl by Henry VI
when they allowed the King to shelter in the castle after his defeat
at the Battle of Towton in 1461. As he handed the bowl over, the
King blessed it and said that as long as it remained unbroken
the Penningtons would flourish. The bowl, called the 'Luck of
Muncaster', has been treasured by the Pennington family for
more than 500 years.

Renwick   When an old church was being demolished here, in the
eighteenth century, a horrid bat-like creature or cockatrice is said
to have flown out of the remains of the building. The people of
Renwick, terrified, barricaded themselves in their homes. One
man only dared to confront the beast – arming himself, first,

with the branch of a rowan tree, traditionally recommended for rendering witches and goblins harmless. It proved effective in this instance.

Souter Fell A phantom army marching over the high ground here was seen by at least twenty people during the early eighteenth century. The army was observed with particular clarity shortly before the rebellion of 1745, leading those who had seen it to conclude that they had witnessed a significant military omen.

Further reading
Armistead, W., *Tales and Legends of the English Lakes*, E.P. Publishing, 1976 (Reprint).
Rowling, Marjorie, *The Folklore of the Lake District*, Batsford, 1976.

Further information from
The Group Librarian, County Library, Tullie House, Castle Street, Carlisle, Cumbria, CA3 8SY.

Derbyshire

Arbor Low There is a stone circle here; its original purpose is as mysterious as that of similar circles in various parts of the country.

Ashbourne A prolonged game of football is played here each year at Shrovetide. The goals are miles away from each other, and much of the action takes place in the local river. It is possible that the origins of the game are ancient, and that it may be an almost unrecognisable form of some fertility ritual.

Barlow Well-dressing ceremonies have been held here. (See **Tissington**, below.)

Beeley A Bronze Age round barrow on the south-west edge of Brampton East Moor is known locally as 'Hob Hurst's House'. Hob – also called, sometimes, 'Hob Thurst' or 'Hob Thrush' – was a bogie or boggart who would secretly make shoes or perform other domestic duties for humans he wished to befriend. The barrow stands on land owned by the Trustees of the Chatsworth Settlement and permission to visit it should be obtained from the Estate Office at Edensor.

Castleton The Garland Day ceremony held here each year at the end of May has been associated during living memory with the Restoration of the Monarchy in 1660, and a 'King' and 'Queen' take part in the festivities. It seems likely, though, that the ceremony may have pre-Christian origins.

Deepdale A cave below Topley Pike is known locally as 'Thirst House' as it was believed to be a home of the elf or goblin Hob Hurst (*cf.* **Beeley**, above). Here, the small creature was supposed to guard a nearby spring which had magical powers of healing.

Derby St Alkmund's Well, in Well Street, has been venerated for the healing powers of its waters. St Mary's Bridge has less happy associations: here, the severed limbs of three executed Roman Catholic priests were exhibited in 1588, and the bridge is said still to re-echo occasionally to the anguished cries of the wretched victims.

Edlaston Well-dressing ceremonies have been held here. (See **Tissington**, below.)

Eldon A pothole here, roughly a mile north of the village of Peak Forest, has been wrongly credited with being bottomless, and with giving the Devil immediate access to the Underworld.

Eyam Well-dressing ceremonies have been held here. (See **Tissington**, below.)

Harthill Moor The stones in the small circle near Robin Hood's Stride have sometimes been called 'The Grey Ladies', because the writers of early guide books used to claim that the boulders came to life and danced together at midnight.

Kinder Scout A pool near Kinder Reservoir, about three miles from Hayfield, is usually known as 'The Mermaid's Pool'. It is said to have some mystical connection with the Atlantic Ocean, and, as its name suggests, to be the haunt of a mermaid. To see this sub-aquatic creature, one is supposed to visit the pool at midnight, just as Easter Sunday begins each year. Anyone fortunate enough to see her will enjoy the secret of eternal life, it is said – though less optimistic accounts say that the viewer is liable to perish that very night. Aaron Ashton, a retired soldier, used to walk annually to the pool from Hayfield without once seeing the mermaid. He died in 1835 at the age of 104.

Morridge The Black Mere near Morridge, between Buxton and Leek, is also said to contain a mermaid, but this one is reputed to be visible any night of the week, at midnight.

Matlock Preserved in the church here (and in some other Derbyshire churches) are garlands that have been carried at the funerals of young unmarried women. These probably have memorial, rather than magical, significance.

Stanton The stones in a small circle here are usually known as 'The Nine Ladies' and the solitary standing stone outside the circle is called 'The King Stone'. According to a centuries-old tale, the ladies were petrified as a punishment for dancing on the Sabbath. The King Stone was their musician.

Stoney Middleton Well-dressing ceremonies have been held here. (See **Tissington**, below.)

Tideswell Well-dressing ceremonies have been held here. (See **Tissington**, below.)

Tissington   The ceremony known as 'Well-dressing' is found now in a number of Derbyshire villages and small towns, but these observances may be of comparatively recent origin. In Tissington, it is known, the five local wells have for centuries been decorated with flowers and garlands.

The custom may have started more or less in its present form as early as AD 1350, when the purity of the local water was given the credit for Tissington's deliverance from the horrors of the Black Death which, in the two previous years, had killed 77 out of the 100 beneficed priests in Derbyshire. It may have originated (or it may have been revived) some 260 years later than this, when the wells of the village continued to provide water of exemplary copiousness and purity through one of the most serious droughts in the country's history. By 1758, Nicholas Hardinge, Clerk of the House of Commons, was writing 'At Tissington . . . we saw the spring adorned with garlands'. The charmingly dressed wells, today, attract many admirers who may not be aware that similar springs were venerated, for their life-giving qualities, thousands of years ago.

Tunstead   An old skull usually referred to as 'Dickey' is kept at a farm between Chapel-en-le-Frith and Whaley Bridge. The skull has been in the house, off and on, for more than three and a half centuries. Several times those occupying the house have tried to get rid of the grim relic, but every time its departure has been followed by crop failures, stock losses, and other disasters. So it has always been resought and brought back.

Winster   A pancake race held here on each Shrove Tuesday may have its origins in some forgotten pre-Christian rite.

Wyaston, Wye Dale and Youlgreave   At these places, Well-dressing ceremonies have recently been observed, reminiscent of the older rites practised at Tissington. (See above.)

Well dressing at Tissington in Derbyshire

Further reading
Rickman, P., *Mysterious Derbyshire*, Dalesman Books, 1977.
Rippon, Anton, *Folktales and Legends of Derbyshire*, Minimax Books, 1982.

Further information from
The County Librarian, County Offices, Matlock, Derbyshire, DE4 3AG.

Devon

Berry Pomeroy   The ruined castle that was once the seat of the powerful Pomeroy family is believed to be haunted. The ghosts, it seems, are Pomeroys who came to unhappy ends and are restless. One ghost who walks through the ruins is said to be a Pomeroy girl who smothered her child, because it had been sired by her father. Another is the beautiful but tragic Margaret Pomeroy who was starved to death by a jealous sister. Seeing either of these ghosts is said to mean the imminent death of the observer.

Bideford   A witch named Temperance Lloyd was accused of sorcery here in 1682, and sent to the gallows with two of her fellows. Unabashed, she proudly claimed that by her craft she had caused the deaths of many Bidefordians.

Braunton The first church here is said to have been founded in the sixth century by St Brannoc, who travelled over the sea from Wales in a stone coffin. He was shown by a sow and her piglets the right place for building the church. Other evidence of St Brannoc's mystical affinity with beasts and birds is offered by carvings inside the present church.

Cadbury Treasure is said to be buried in the hill fort known as 'Cadbury Castle', and in Dolbury Hill some five miles away. A fiery dragon, trusty keeper of both these hoards, was believed in the Middle Ages to fly at night-time to and fro between the two hills.

Chagford More than three centuries ago, Whiddon Park was the home of a girl called Mary Whiddon. When she went to Chagford Church to be married, she was shot and killed by a young man who was jealous of her husband-to-be. Her ghost has occasionally been seen in her old home.

Dartmoor Several places in this relatively wild area are said to be the homes of evil spirits – Cranmere Pool, near its northern borders, is as phantom-ridden as any. On Fox Tor is, reputedly, the tomb of a Saxon nobleman named Childe who was lost on Dartmoor after a day's hunting. Overtaken by a blizzard, he was forced to kill his horse and to cut his way into it for shelter and warmth. On a stone nearby he wrote with the horse's blood a will leaving his lands to whomever should find and bury his body.

In the valley of the West Dart, not far from Two Bridges, the gnarled old oaks of Wistman's Wood have been said, for many decades, to be haunted by a pack of savage Wish Hounds, used by the Devil for hunting humans. The River Dart, too, is reputed to be supernaturally dangerous. A couplet well known in the neighbourhood threatens:

> River Dart, River of Dart,
> Every year thou claimest a heart.

Records show that this small but unpredictable watercourse has indeed a high record of mortality.

Down St Mary A ghostly black dog is said locally to wander through this village at night.

Exeter St Sidwell's Well, just outside the city, is one of several in England and Wales associated with the martyrdom of a virtuous girl, many centuries ago. In this instance the maiden had inherited some land, which her jealous stepmother wanted. Under orders from the covetous woman, two harvesters cut off the head of the girl as she knelt in prayer. Water sprang from the ground where the severed head came to rest.

Exmoor The church bells of Withypool were too much for the local fairies to put up with, some say, so the wee folk moved out of earshot. Other places on and by Exmoor are said to be particularly favoured by gnomes and goblins.

Halwell There is a 'holy' or healing well here.

Hartland Point This was the home, during the sixth century, of the Welsh mystic called St Nectan. The saint is supposed to have been attacked by robbers, who cut off his head. Unperturbed, Nectan picked up his head and walked with it to the well now named after him. Wherever his blood dropped, on the journey, foxgloves grew out of the ground. The saint's memory has been honoured for many years by children carrying foxgloves on St Nectan's Day, 17 June.

Hatherleigh Early in each November, blazing tar barrels have traditionally been drawn through the streets of the town, recalling the pre-Christian autumn festivities that were probably held here.

Kingsteignton The roasting of a ram in the town in spring is similarly held to recall some ancient sacrifice, made to restore the local water supply.

Lydford   The ruins of the castle are said to be haunted by several ghosts. The infamous Judge Jeffreys is believed to turn up here from time to time, appropriately disguised as a black pig. Other spectres seen on the site may remind the sensitive of the many prisoners executed here without a fair trial. As William Browne of Tavistock (1590–1643) wrote:

> I oft have heard of Lydford law,
> How in the morn they hang and draw,
> And sit in judgment after.

North Tawton   A dry depression in a field near Cottle's Wood is said to fill inexplicably with water when national security is threatened, or when a great public hero is about to die.

Ottery St Mary   The fire ceremonies held here can be compared with those of Hatherleigh (q.v.).

Plymouth   Associations with Sir Francis Drake abound in the district. At Devil's Point, it is said, Drake met Satan and exchanged his soul for a tempest that would drive the Spanish fleet to destruction. A tangible reminder of Drake is his drum, still cherished in Buckland Abbey. Ghostly reverberations can be heard from this drum at times of national emergency, or so it is believed.

Shaugh Bridge   The Devil is said to hunt with his ghostly Wish Hounds around Dewerstone Rock. Any human silly enough to become a hunt supporter of this pack is liable to be led to the Dewerstone. The line, after that, involves a steep and potentially fatal drop to the river.

Shebbear   There is a large boulder in the Square, under which the Devil is reputed to lie.

Tavistock   The ghost of a Lady Howard, born in 1596, is said to drive out occasionally through the Fitzford Gate, all that now remains of her ancestral home. In her macabre coach drawn by headless horses, she is said to travel to Okehampton Church and back. The real-life Lady Howard had four husbands, some of whom she is alleged to have murdered.

Totnes Set in the pavement of Fore Street here is a large boulder known as 'The Brutus Stone'. On to this, according to legend, the great survivor of the siege of Troy stepped when he first landed in Britain. Shortly after that, he is said to have captured Gog and Magog, two of the local giants. He took them with him to London to act as his personal bodyguards.

Uplyme The Black Dog Inn here, as its name suggests, is said to be visited by the ghostly quadruped that roams through so many country towns and villages.

Woolacombe Several villages near here are said to be haunted by the ghost of Sir William de Tracy, one of the four knights who assassinated Thomas à Becket at Canterbury. (Sir William hailed from nearby Mortehoe.) The ghost tends to be particularly active and audible in rough weather, justifying the local belief that the Tracys 'had ever the wind and the rain in their faces'.

Zeal Monachorum Members of the Oxenham family who lived here centuries ago are said to have been visited by a large white-breasted bird almost immediately before they were due to die. Later heads of the family are said to have been treated to the same sign – in one instance, as far away from Zeal Monachorum as Earl's Terrace, in Kensington.

Further reading
Jellicoe and Mayne, *The Shell Guide to Devon*, Faber, New Edition 1982.

Further information from
The County Librarian, Central Library, Castle Street, Exeter, EX4 3PQ.

Dorset

Abbotsbury   As late as the end of the nineteenth century, the fisherfolk of this Dorset town used to take floral decorations out to sea on a prescribed day in each May, and then throw them overboard – presumably to appease some ancient god of the sea. Flower-bearing Abbotsburians have walked in procession round the town more recently, but their offerings have usually been left at the local war memorial.

Athelhampton   The ancient dwelling known as 'Athelhampton House' is said to harbour numerous ghosts. A phantom cooper is sometimes heard hammering on non-existent barrels that were once stored in the cellar next to the Great Hall. Ghostly duellists have been reported. The strangest shade, perhaps, takes the form of a monkey. This is believed to be a pet that once belonged to members of the Martyn family, early owners of the house. Once when a Martyn girl was disappointed in love she went up a secret staircase to a concealed room. There she closed the door, not realising that the family monkey had been following her, and committed suicide. The monkey, unable to escape from the staircase, died of starvation.

Badbury Rings   This Iron Age hill fort is one of the places at which King Arthur may finally have defeated the Saxons in the sixth century. Early historians claimed that he achieved this victory by carrying a Christian cross on his shoulders for three days and three nights.

Batcombe   In this manor, in the sixteenth century, there lived a squire named Mynterne who was a notorious wizard, or 'conjuror'. Before he died, Squire Mynterne expressed a wish that he should be buried 'neither within the church nor without it'. So his tomb was constructed in such a way that half his body lies inside the church walls, and the other half in 'God's Acre'.

Bettiscombe An ancient skull kept in Bettiscombe Manor cannot be got rid of – or so it is said – without great unhappiness affecting the occupants of the house and, almost inevitably, damage to the fabric.

Bincombe The early settlements on Bincombe Down and Bincombe Hill are recalled by numerous barrows or burial mounds. These are said to have been, in recent centuries, the homes of fairies with musical tastes. Melodies played or sung by the little hidden artistes are believed to be most audible around midday.

Cerne Abbas The giant male figure cut in the chalk hillside near Cerne Abbas has obvious associations with fertility. Maypole dances were held above the figure until the seventeenth century, and less formal celebrations of courtship and love are said still to continue on the high ground, around Midsummer.

Flowers Barrow Roman legionaries who once occupied this Iron Age earthwork are said still to appear occasionally, carrying out their phantom defensive duties.

Halstock The name of the Quiet Woman Inn recalls the local saintly female called Juthware or Judith who, some twelve centuries ago, was beheaded by a jealous brother. Stoically, the victim is said to have picked up her head and carried it to Halstock Church before she died. Her ghost has been seen on Judith Hill.

Kingston The Scott Arms is said to be haunted by the ghost of an elderly woman.

Lyme Regis After the Duke of Monmouth's ill-fated rebellion, Judge Jeffreys conducted the infamous 'Bloody Assize' in this area. Jeffreys's ghost is still said to be seen occasionally in Lyme Regis, where twelve of the local people were hanged.

Cerne Abbas

Poole The Crown Hotel is one of several buildings in the town reputed to be haunted.

Shaftesbury The ghost of a monk has been seen where the ancient abbey used to stand. Some say that the monk alone knew the secret of the abbey's hidden treasure.

Sherborne The ghost of Sir Walter Raleigh is believed to haunt the grounds of Sherborne Castle.

Shillingstone This was one of the last places in Dorset to have a horned mask, worn in ritual dances by an 'Ooser' – a survivor, probably, of some figure that took part in pagan fertility rituals. A mask that had survived at Melbury Osmond disappeared at the beginning of this century, but it had been photographed, and a new mask was made at Weymouth in 1973.

Spettisbury A witch who once lived here was said to be able to immobilise cattle by staring at them. She earned a good living by demanding payments for averting her gaze.

Stalbridge This place has been renowned for its witches, the most notable being the kindly Mother Hurn, who dispensed prophecies and magical remedies.

Ulwell This was the home of the old witch Jinny Gould, who lived near a toll gate. Late one night, a drunken traveller saw a cat sitting on the gate, so he whipped it. On the following day, Jinny was found dead, with a lacerated back. After that, the gate was said to open without human aid whenever a late night wayfarer approached.

Whitchurch Canonicorum In the church is the shrine of St Wite. The shrine, built in the thirteenth century, is pierced with holes. Into these, ailing pilgrims would put their arms or legs, confident that the saint's far-famed powers would benefit them.

Wimborne   Witches used to meet at Leigh Common, near here, to perform malign rituals with wax images. The magistrates became so incensed that they waylaid the women and ducked them in the local ponds.

Wool   A ghostly coach-and-four is said to drive at midnight from Woolbridge Manor, but it can only be seen by descendants of the Turberville family, who used to live in the house.

Further reading
Chadwick, John C., *Folklore and Witchcraft in Dorset and Wiltshire*, N.J. Clarke Publications, Lyme Regis, 1984.

Further information from
The Assistant Reference Librarian (Local Studies), County Library, Colliton Park, Dorchester, DT1 1XJ.

Durham

Bishopton   Castle Hill, which was raised during the twelfth century, has for many years been occupied by fairies, or so it is said in the district. Local folk attempting to remove its earth have been told by mysterious voices to 'leave the Fairy Hill alone'.

Darlington   Deep pools near the River Tees are known as 'Hell's Kettles'. (There are similar water-filled depressions in the red sandstone banks on the east side of the River Ure.) Holinshed, in his *Chronicles of England*, published in 1577, said that people called them that, as if the Devil 'should seethe souls of sinful men and women in them'. The cries of the tormented are said often to have been heard coming from the 'Kettles'. W. Hylton Dyer Longstaffe, author of *The History and Antiquities of the Parish of Darlington*, published in 1854, tells how a local farmer once insisted on working on St Barnabas' Day, when more reverent people would have rested. On being rebuked, the farmer, eager to get to his hayfield, retorted:

> 'I'll hae my cart load of hay
> Whether God will or nay'.

At that, the Hell's Kettles swallowed the farmer and, with him, his carts and his horses. A reader of the *Durham Advertiser* has claimed that they may be seen on a fine day, when the water is clear, 'floating midway, many fathoms deep'.

Durham   The buildings on the north side of Elvet Bridge are said to have been haunted by the restless spirit of an old piper who was brought down the river during a flood, and on being taken alive from the foaming waters, lived for some years in a house of correction on the site.

Jarrow   A tall, straight-backed, rudely-hewn chair in St Paul's Church is said to have belonged to the Venerable Bede, who lived for many years in Jarrow. Mysterious powers have been attributed over the centuries to the timbers of this ancient seat – 'Many a fair lady has borne away, in the past, chippings of this wonder-working relic, to place them under pillow, confident that the man she dreams of, under so powerful a charm, is destined to be her husband', reported the local historian mentioned above. Brides would ask to be allowed to sit in the chair, to make sure that their marriages would be fertile. Pregnant women soaked slivers of wood from the chair in water, believing that if they drank the resulting fluid they would suffer less, when giving birth. With so many virtues ascribed to Bede's chair, it is remarkable that any of the original wood has survived to the present day.

Pelton   A small village near here was once said to be the home of a mischievous goblin known as 'The Picktree Brag'. The brag used to appear to the villagers in a number of different guises –

sometimes it would resemble a coach horse; at other times, an ass. One ninety-year-old woman distinctly heard the goblin, which at the time appeared like a calf with a white handkerchief about its neck, and a bushy tail, 'settin' up a great nicker and a whinney every now and then'.

Penshaw The Lambtons of Lambton Castle, near here, suffered tragic misfortunes through at least seven generations, after being cursed by a witch. Their troubles started when a young male Lambton, fishing in the River Wear one Sunday, hooked and landed a curious small dragon or 'worm'. He put the worm in a well by the castle, and then forgot all about it. By the time he returned from crusading in the Holy Land, the worm had grown so big that it could coil itself three times round Lambton Hill, and was the terror of the district. After taking advice from the local witch, the young Lambton fitted his armour with razor-sharp blades, and met the worm in mortal combat in the middle of the river. In exchange for her advice, the warrior had promised that he would kill the first creature to greet him after the hoped-for victory. All went more or less according to plan, and the worm cut itself to pieces on the knight's deadly knives. But instead of sending one of the family's hounds to greet the worm's conqueror, as previously arranged, the knight's father himself rushed down to the riverside. The knight refused to kill his father and, for this, the family was cursed.

Sedgefield An unorthodox football match which has been played here for many years at Shrovetide may have untraceable pre-Christian origins.

Sockburn Here, as at **Penshaw** (see above), the district was terrorised in the Middle Ages by a ferocious dragon. The 'Sockburn Worm' was reputedly killed by a Sir John Conyers, who managed to attack it at its only vulnerable spot – under one of its wings. A large grey stone in a field by Sockburn Church is said to show where the creature met its end.

Whitburn   Many bridal couples leaving the church here after the marriage ceremony have been given spiced and mulled ale to drink. The origins of this ancient custom are obscure.

Further reading
Brockie, William, *Legends and Superstitions of the County of Durham*, E.P. Publishing Ltd, 1974 (Reprint)

Further information from
The Divisional Librarian, Durham County Library (Durham City Branch), South Street, Durham, DH1 4QS.

East Sussex

Alfriston   St Andrew's Church was built in the fourteenth century in the form of a cross. The site for the church is popularly supposed to have been indicated by four white oxen, which miraculously appeared at the village and lay down together, forming a cross, with their heads outwards.

Battle   The soil in the fields over which the Battle of Hastings was fought in 1066 is said still to exude blood after rain has fallen on it. The presence of iron in the soil suggests a more mundane reason for the discoloration of local puddles.

Brede   Brede Place was said by Sir Edwin Lutyens to be the most haunted inhabited house in Sussex. One of the old mansion's owners – Sir Goddard Oxenbridge – earned the reputation, in the district, of being an eater of babies. At last, in 1537, the villagers waylaid him when he was drunk, on Groaning Bridge, and cut his body in half with a wooden saw. He is said to haunt both the bridge and Brede Place.

Brighton   Several ghosts are said to enhance the night life of this popular resort. By St Nicholas' Church, for instance, a horse once ridden by an armour-clad warrior is said to reappear on moonlit nights, and the shade of a monk who was starved to death for breaking his vows of celibacy is reputed to pass through a brick wall in Meeting House Lane.

Buxted   Nan Tuck's Lane and Tuck's Wood are said to be haunted by the ghost of a simple girl who may have committed suicide in 1661, after being accused of witchcraft and cruelly persecuted.

Crowborough   For a long time, Jarvis Brook Road was believed to be haunted by a bag of soot which, like some other malevolent spectres, was prone to chase startled travellers.

Herstmonceux   Several ghosts have been reported from the Castle, built by Sir Roger de Fiennes in 1440. Best known is the phantom drummer who was believed to walk the battlements, producing eerie, paranormal sounds. Some said that one elderly owner of the Castle staged this ghostly manifestation in order to scare younger, more virile neighbours away from his lovable wife.

Hollington   The 'Church in the Wood', here, is supposed to have been moved by the Devil to a place that Christians would find hard to reach.

Lewes   The fire ceremonies held here annually on 5 November are probably continuing reminders of pagan rites, as well as commemorating the Protestant inhabitants of the town who were burned to death for their beliefs during the reign of Mary Tudor.

Mayfield   St Dunstan, working here as a blacksmith, is said to have been visited by the Devil, who was disguised as a beautiful woman. The Devil tried in vain to tempt the saint, but Dunstan kept working. Then he noticed cloven hoofs beneath the 'woman's' skirts. Taking his red-hot tongs (still preserved in Mayfield's Old Palace), he gripped the Devil's nose. The Devil, in his agony, is said to have plunged into a pool at Tunbridge Wells, which explains why the spa water there is reddish and tastes of brimstone.

Michelham The gatehouse at the Augustinian Priory is said to have been haunted for many years by a Grey Lady.

Rotherfield Mysterious footsteps have been heard in the King's Arms – usually late in June, and invariably in the evening.

Rye Phantom monks are said to have been seen at Monastery Hall (at one time an Augustinian friary) and on Watch-hill Street.

South Heighton After some ancient ilex trees were felled here, early in this century, the house nearby was haunted so disturbingly that no one would live in it. Then the vicar carried out a service of exorcism in the deserted rooms. This seemed to be effective.

Wilmington The Long Man cut in the turf on the north face of Windover Hill is probably between two and three thousand years old and may have been put here to represent some long-forgotten god of war. The origins of the figure are, however, a matter of conjecture.

Winchelsea The Queen's Head Hotel, formerly a farmhouse, is said to be haunted. The shade is either that of a tenant farmer who once lived in the building, or of a publican who died in it, and whose body was exhibited, to his former customers, in the bar.

Further reading
Simpson, Jacqueline, *Folklore of Sussex*, Batsford, 1973.

Herstmonceux Castle, haunted by a drummer

Further information from
The Reference Team Librarian (Local Studies), Brighton Central
    Library, Church Street, Brighton, BN1 1UE; and The Reference
    Team Librarian, Hastings Central Library, 13 Claremont,
    Hastings, TN34 1HE.

Essex

Ashingdon   This is now supposed to be the site of the great battle
fought in October 1016 between the Danish invader King Cnut
and the English King Edmund Ironside. The victorious Cnut is
believed to have built St Andrew's Church over the graves of
the enemies his men had slain. No grass would grow on the
bloodstained hill for centuries afterwards, if tradition is to be
believed. Cnut's men who had died in battle were buried under
the round barrows known as 'The Bartlow Hills'. Here, the dwarf
elder (*Sambucus ebulus*) has since then flourished profusely.
The name given to it locally – 'Danes'-blood' – suggests the
nourishment alleged to give the stems, leaves and fruit their
characteristic colour in autumn.

Basildon   The Church of the Holy Cross is said to be haunted by
a ghostly priest, clad in scarlet robes.

Borley   The Rectory, built in 1863, soon became notorious for the
persistence of the ghosts reputed to haunt it. Most poignant of
all was the wild-eyed nun Marie Lairre who had been either
strangled or walled up alive and left to perish of starvation. After
prolonged investigations were carried out into the hauntings, the
Rectory was mysteriously burned to the ground early in 1938.
The hauntings are said to have continued even after the rubble
had been cleared from the site.

Canewdon This is one of the many towns in Essex which are alleged to have housed wizards and witches. Here, until early in this century, the local farmers were required to pay 'protection money' to practitioners of the Black Arts.

Chelmsford Witches – or supposed witches – were tried and hanged in considerable numbers in Chelmsford during the sixteenth and seventeenth centuries. The infamous witch-finder Matthew Hopkins, who claimed that he had in his possession 'The Devil's list of all English witches', is said to have brought as many as nineteen wretched old women to grievous ends in Chelmsford in a single day.

Coggeshall The site of the former Abbey Church here has been visited from time to time by the ghost of a monk. There is also a local ghost known as 'Robin the Woodcutter'. Robin is supposed to have been a sculptor of some competence whose best work mysteriously disappeared at the time of the Reformation.

Danbury The Church of St John the Baptist was visited by the Devil early in the fifteenth century, according to the *Historia Anglica* printed at Walsingham in 1653. The Evil One, disguised as a Grey Friar, did considerable damage to the fabric of the church before he disappeared.

Epping The old earthworks known as 'Amesbury Banks' deep in Epping Forest are allegedly haunted by the ghosts of Queen Boudicca and her daughters.

Henham According to a pamphlet published in the seventeenth century, Henham was once visited by a winged dragon, or 'Flying Serpent'. Strong ale known as 'Snakebite' became much favoured in the district after that.

Little Baddow A door in the north wall of Little Baddow Church is popularly known as 'The Devil's Door'. It leads from the interior of the church to that part of the surrounding land the Devil was supposed to favour.

Manningtree Here, in the early seventeenth century, Matthew Hopkins practised unsuccessfully as a lawyer. Later, he became famous in his self-appointed capacity of 'Witch-finder General'. (See **Chelmsford, Essex,** above.)

Rochford Anne Boleyn is said to have been born at Rochford Hall. (Several other places claim the honour). The executed Queen's ghost is said to revisit this reputed birthplace at Christmas.

Sible Hedingham Here, as late as 1863, an octogenarian who was deaf and dumb was accused of witchcraft. The villagers, believing that the old man had been casting spells, pulled him from the bar of the Swan Inn and threw him into the stream nearby, to see if he would float. This, according to witch-hunting lore, would prove that the old man was guilty of sorcery. He was pulled from the water by some of his more charitable neighbours before the matter could be settled either way, but he died a few days later, probably as a result of the treatment he had received.

One bedroom in the Bell Inn at Sible Hedingham is said to be haunted by the ghost of a teen-age girl with long black hair.

St Osyth Here, in 1921, two skeletons were disinterred from unconsecrated ground in the village. The elbows and knees of both had been pinned, before burial, with big iron rivets. Experts judged that the bones were probably those of two elderly females who had been executed for allegedly practising witchcraft. The rivets were intended to forestall the possibility of any later hauntings, by either of the pair.

Theydon Bois Hill Hall is said to have been haunted at various times by the ghosts of a black dog, an old lady, and a coachman driving a team of phantom horses.

Tolleshunt Knights The Devil is said to have been fond of attending wild revels by a bottomless pool here. His pleasures were threatened when workmen started to build a house close by. A watchman instructed to guard the site tried to protect himself from supernatural interference by taking along his three spayed bitches, but these failed to have the required effect. The workman's heart is said to have been buried, to save his soul from the Devil, somewhere within the walls of the local church.

Further reading
Day, James Wentworth, *Essex Ghosts*, Spur Books, 1973.
Morgan, Glyn, *Essex Witches*, Spur Books, 1973.
Morgan, Glyn, *Secret Essex*, Ian Henry, 1982.

Further information from
The Local Studies Librarian, Central Library, Trinity Square, Colchester, CO1 1JR.

Gloucestershire

Berkeley According to William of Malmesbury, writing early in the twelfth century, Berkeley had recently been the home of a rich woman who was addicted to witchcraft. Warned, one day, by her pet jackdaw that she was about to suffer some dreadful calamity, she was told almost immediately that her son and his whole family had been killed. Realising that the bird had been right, and that her own end was at hand, she told her remaining children to wrap her body in the skin of a stag and to put it in a stone coffin, secured with three iron chains. The coffin was then to be kept in the local church until sufficient psalms had been said over it, after which it could be safely buried outside, in consecrated ground. The lady's precautions were useless, for demons snapped the chains, smashed the coffin and dragged her out of the church. At the door a black horse was waiting with iron hooks all over its back. The pitiable cries sent up by the lady as she was carried away on the horse were heard for miles. So, too, were the screams of Edward II, foully murdered in Berkeley

Castle in 1327. Strange disturbances are said to be heard in the locality to this day.

Cirencester William Budden, writing in 1685, reported that two men digging for gravel in Torbarrow Hill had found there a mysterious cavern, richly furnished, in which was an armed man, guarding some treasure by the light of an ever-burning lamp. The intruders had just enough time to observe two embalmed heads, with long beards, before the armed man managed to extinguish his flame. As soon as the scared mortals had escaped from the cavern the earth fell in and buried all its contents.

Deerhurst The country round Deerhurst was said by Sir Robert Atkins, writing in 1712, to have been plagued, during the Middle Ages, by a 'serpent of prodigious bigness', which poisoned the local people and killed their cattle. The serpent, or dragon, was eventually killed by one John Smith, a labourer, who was rewarded for his daring by the gift of a local estate.

Fairford In earlier centuries, the town is said to have been the home of some particularly malicious witches, whose ghosts are believed still to haunt the Poulton crossroads, where, in life, the witches played some of their most spectacular tricks.

Forest of Dean This sparsely-populated, well-wooded district has been for at least four centuries one of the favourite haunts of the leading gipsy families of southern Britain. Gipsies found in the Forest are famed for their knowledge of, and proficiency in, magical practices and divination.

Gloucester A tailor who once lived and worked in this ancient city fell sick. Then he found that his unfinished tasks were completed for him, while he slept, by benevolent elves. When Beatrix Potter, staying in the city, heard this story she used it,

The mysterious yews at Painswick

after some revision, as the basis of one of her most enchanting tales.

Painswick The clipped yew trees in the churchyard at Painswick are famous. According to a local tradition there are ninety-nine of them, and attempts made to grow a hundredth tree have always been doomed to failure. Ceremonies associated with yew-clipping that have been held in the churchyard are believed to have mysterious pre-Christian origins.

Prestbury This – once the home of the successful but tormented jockey Fred Archer – is reputed to be the most haunted village in Gloucestershire.

Tintern A large stone near the ruined abbey is said to have been put there by the Devil, so that from it he could spy on the Abbot and the other members of Tintern's monastic community.

Whittington Sir Laurence Tanfield, an unscrupulous local landowner, has been believed, since his death in the seventeenth century, to take rides in the district in a ghostly coach drawn by four black horses. To see Sir Laurence on one of his journeys is said to have fatal consequences for the unlucky observer.

Winchcombe Two stone coffins in the parish church are thought to be those of two Saxon kings – Kenulf, King of Mercia, who founded Winchcombe Abbey in the eighth century, and his son Kenelm, who succeeded him. When Kenelm, still a boy, was murdered by his tutor, acting on the instructions of Kenelm's elder sister, a dove that flew miraculously from Gloucestershire to Italy is believed to have alerted the Pope, in Rome, to the young king's fate. The Pope then told all the other English kings to take action to avenge Kenelm's death. Kenelm's wicked sister tried to counteract this by reciting backwards the 'cursing psalm' (Psalm 108). The ruse did not work, and the misguided girl died in dreadful agony.

Further reading
Price, Merlin, *Folktales and Legends of Gloucestershire*, Minimax
   Books, Peterborough, 1984.

Further information from
The Divisional Librarian, Gloucester Library, Brunswick Road,
   Gloucester, GL1 1HT.

Greater London

Chiswick   Walpole House is said to be haunted by the ghost of
Barbara, Duchess of Cleveland, once the mistress of Charles II.
She revisits her former home in the guise of a sad, swollen old
lady, lamenting the lost looks of her youth.

Drury Lane   The Theatre Royal is reputed to be haunted by the
ghost of the comedian Dan Leno and by a phantom man in grey.
The reappearance of the latter wraith is believed to herald success
for the play being currently staged.

Ely Place   On his way to be executed, St Blaise is said to have
stopped to save the life of a child who was choking on a fishbone.
In St Ethelreda's Church here, on St Blaise's Day, a priest blesses
children suffering from diseases of the throat.

Garlic Hill   The church of St James is said to be haunted by a
ghost clad in a misty shroud.

Ham   The ghost of Elizabeth, Duchess of Lauderdale, reputed to
have killed her first husband so that she could marry her second,
has been seen and heard at Ham House. Her silver-topped ebony
cane taps restlessly along the mansion's dark corridors.

Hampton Court The Palace is said to be haunted by two important ghosts. Lady Jane Seymour is reputed to wander about the Queen's Apartments, carrying a lighted taper. Queen Katherine Howard's screams and pleas for mercy echo in vain. down the Haunted Gallery. Other less noteworthy supernatural visitors have been reported.

Kensington The grounds of Holland House, which was nearly destroyed by bombing in World War Two, are reputed to be haunted by the headless ghost of a seventeenth-century Lord Holland, beheaded for the part he played in the Civil War.

Mortlake Doctor John Dee – magician, adviser in supernatural matters to Elizabeth I, and notorious conjurer-up of spirits – used to live by the Parish Church, and is buried here.

Primrose Hill Here, and at Parliament Hill Fields, groups of bards, druids and ovates have, in modern times, attempted to reproduce the rituals of their ancient predecessors.

Richmond As Elizabeth I lay dying in the gatehouse of the old palace by the Green, a horseman waited below the window of her room for instructions to ride towards Scotland with her ring – a sign to James VI of that country that he had become King of England, too. The echoing hoofbeats of the horse galloping away after the ring had been dropped from the window are still occasionally heard.

Soho A house in Dean Street is said to be haunted by the ghost of Nell Gwyn – orange-seller, actress, and mistress of Charles II – who once lived in the building.

Tottenham Bruce Castle, once a school, is said to be haunted by the ghost of a seventeenth-century lady who was shut up, by her jealous husband, in the clock tower. On the anniversary of the lady's suicide, in early November, wild screams are allegedly heard.

Tower of London   Many ghosts are said to have appeared in this grim stronghold – the shades of those such as Anne Boleyn and Lady Jane Grey who have died by the axe being, understandably, the most persistent.

Further information from
The Museum of London, 150 London Wall, London, EC2.
The Guildhall Library, Guildhall, London, EC2.

Greater Manchester

Blackley   In 1844 Samuel Bamford described, in his *Passages in the Life of a Radical*, 'a rather deep valley', near Blackley, 'green swarded, and embowered in plantations and woods'. This gorge had been known, and still was, he said, as 'Boggart Ho' or 'The glen of the hall of the spirits'. All traces of the ancient dwelling of a 'sly and strange elf' or 'boggart' described by Bamford seem to have vanished now from Boggart Hole Clough, but the place is still associated with mystery and magic.

Bolton   At Smithills Hall, near here, a Protestant named George Marsh was interrogated in 1555. Following that, he was burned at the stake at Boughton in Cheshire. The ghost of this unhappy martyr is said to have since been seen at the Hall, and a depression that is said to be the imprint of his foot can be clearly seen in a domestic flagstone.

Bury   At Unsworth, about three miles from Bury, a dragon is said to have devoured many women and children. The beast was killed when the owner of the manor house loaded his gun with his dagger and mortally wounded his quarry in the throat.

Radcliffe   According to John Harland, writing in 1882, the Tower at Radcliffe was haunted for centuries by a black dog. This, he suggested, may have been a reminder of the girl called 'Fair Ellen of Radcliffe' who, by orders of her jealous stepmother, was murdered, cut up, and served at dinner as 'venison pasty' to her father.

Rochdale St Chad's Church, built on a hill, was originally meant to be sited on low-lying ground by the River Roach, or so it is said. The materials were moved overnight, by supernatural means, to the church's present location.

Worsley In Wardley Hall there is a skull which belonged, it is said by some, to Roger Downes, a wild and debauched courtier of Charles II's reign. Killed in a brawl – probably on or near London Bridge – Downes had his head cut off. It was sent, in a box, to his sister at Wardley. Other authorities claim the skull to be that of a priest executed in Manchester in 1641. Whichever is true, the skull is said to have a marked aversion to being moved from this resting-place.

Further information from
The County Librarian, County Hall, Piccadilly Gardens, Portland
   Street, Manchester, M60 3HP.

Hampshire

Basing The mansion known as 'Basing House' was first besieged and then blown up by Parliamentary forces during the Civil War. Among the ghosts said to haunt the locality are the shades of Cromwell and of an unidentified Cavalier.

Beaulieu In the ruins of Beaulieu Abbey, founded in 1204, the voices of singing monks are allegedly heard.

Bisterne A 'devouring Dragon' that once lived near here is said to have been slain by a Sir Maurice de Berkeley.

Braishfield   The land round a cottage in Dark Lane is said to be haunted by the ghost of a rich woman who once lived in the district. She is believed to be looking for some treasure that she hid shortly before she died.

Burley   On the Beacon, near here, lived the dragon said to have been killed at **Bisterne** (see above). It used to fly down to Bisterne with distressing regularity to ask for a bucket of milk.

Chilbolton   The Rectory, here, is said to be visited occasionally by a ghostly nurse-like figure. This may be the shade of a nun who lived in the fourteenth century in the Benedictine Abbey at Wherwell. She is said to have broken her vows, and to have run away from the abbey. When she gave herself up, years later, she is said to have been walled up alive in the nunnery which stood, then, on the site of the present Chilbolton Rectory.

Ellingham   Moyles Court is said to be haunted by the ghost of Dame Alice Lisle, who, though more than seventy years old, was beheaded in Winchester in 1685, having been found guilty of harbouring two men on the run, after the Battle of Sedgemoor.

Liphook   Two ghosts are popularly supposed to haunt the lanes and fields around Liphook – a phantom that looks like a lively white calf, and the shade of a small boy who occasionally appears, playing a flute.

Owslebury   Henry VIII married Jane Seymour in Marwell Hall, a little to the south of Owslebury. Within twelve months, she was dead, having failed to survive the birth of her son, later to be King Edward VI. The queen's ghost is said still to be seen in Marwell Hall, and an avenue of trees near the building is believed to be haunted occasionally by her royal predecessor, Anne Boleyn.

Portsmouth   James or Jack Aitken was hanged at the entrance to Portsmouth Harbour in 1776. He held subversive views, and he had been caught trying to set fire to part of the dockyard. After the execution, his body was exhibited in a gibbet on Blockhouse Point. His chains can still be heard clanking on windy nights, or so it is believed.

Southampton A long barrow on Ports Down has been called for centuries 'Bevis's Grave'. Sir Bevis, hero of the district in times gone by, is said to have killed the giant Ascapart, who was causing much trouble in the neighbourhood. The statue on Southampton's medieval Bar Gate which is often said to represent Sir Bevis is, in fact, a portrait of George III clad in the clothes of Ancient Rome.

Vernham Dean When plague threatened the inhabitants of this place in 1665, the Rector persuaded all those who might have become infected to leave the village, and to isolate themselves in a camp on top of a nearby hill. To make their exile possible, he promised to take them food at regular intervals. Unfortunately for the outcasts, the Rector's resolution failed, and those on the hill who did not become mortally sick perished of starvation. The cowardly clergyman's ghost has often been seen since, making the journey that he was too scared to make when he was alive.

Wherwell This place is supposed to have been the haunt, during the Middle Ages, of a cockatrice – a winged monster that lived principally on human flesh. The beast was tackled eventually, by a man called Green, who is said to have introduced a sheet of polished metal into its lair. The cockatrice fought with its own reflection until it was quite exhausted. Green was then able to kill the monster without much difficulty. He was rewarded with the gift of some land in nearby Harewood Forest. The ground he was given is still referred to, locally, as 'Green's Acres'.

Winchester The ninth-century Bishop of Winchester named 'Swithun' wished to be buried, after his death, where rain would fall on his grave. Some years after he had been interred in the Cathedral's grounds, the local monks decided that the interior of the building would provide a more suitable resting-place for

Swithun's bones. The exhumation that they then set in hand proved disastrous – the saint showed his disapproval of the move by sending rain, almost continuously, for forty days and forty nights. Since then, rain falling on St Swithun's Day has been taken to portend more than a month of abnormally bad weather.

Further reading
Boase, Wendy, *The Folklore of Hampshire and the Isle of Wight*, Batsford, 1976.

Further information from
The County Librarian, County Library Headquarters, 81 North Walls, Winchester, SO23 8BY.

Herefordshire and Worcestershire

Aconbury   The water from St Anne's Well here is said to be of great benefit to those suffering from diseases of the eye. In previous centuries, it was thought to be particularly effective if taken from the well at midnight on Twelfth Night.

Besford   A man who owned a pack of hounds and who kept them at Church Farm here was disturbed one night by the noise they were making. So he sent his kennelman to calm them. The kennelman did not return. Next morning his body was found, in a partly devoured state. Now, on dark nights, the late kennelman's boots are believed to stride spectrally across the field ('Dog Kennel Piece') on which the tragedy occurred, and ghostly hounds can be heard giving tongue.

Brampton Bryan   On 3 September 1658–the day on which Oliver Cromwell died – there was a great storm that brought down numerous trees in Brampton Bryan Park. Local people said that the Devil must have passed through the park as he dragged the dead Protector down to Hell. It is still believed in the district that Satan returns to Brampton Bryan each year, on the anniversary of Cromwell's death, to re-enact, with Cromwell's shade, the grim scene.

Brinsop   There is evidence in Brinsop that St George may have killed the dragon in this parish. Most striking is the carved tablet set in the north wall of the church. A well just to the south of the church has been known for centuries as 'The Dragon's Well'.

Bromsgrove   The boar's head seen in the coat of arms of the local council is supposed to recall the monster slain by the legendary Sir Ryalas. After he had killed the boar, Sir Ryalas discovered that the beast was really the son of a fiendish sorceress, so he killed her, too.

Callow   Nearly two hundred years ago, a number of people who were travelling by coach were murdered at an overnight stopping-place on Callow Hill. The house in which their bodies were found has long since disappeared, but a phantom version of it is said to have been visible from time to time.

Clodock   St Clodack's Church here is dedicated to the memory of a sixth-century ruler who, through no fault of his own, came to a violent end. When the oxen drawing the saint's body to a suitable place of interment reached the River Monnow, they halted and refused to move forward. This was taken as a sign from Heaven that Clodack should be buried by the side of the river, and that a church should be built over his grave.

Colwall   A big boulder here is said locally to have been deposited in Colwall by the Devil, but nobody seems to know why he left it.

Goodrich   The ruined Norman castle at Goodrich is said to be haunted by the ghosts of a pair of ill-fated lovers who tried to escape from its walls while the stronghold was being besieged by

Ruined Goodrich Castle, by the Wye

Parliamentary forces during the Civil War. The lovers were
drowned in the Wye, which their spirits still attempt to cross,
even today, but vainly.

Hereford   Near the entrance to Castle Green, there was once a
well. (Its site can still be identified.) According to tradition, this
well came into existence when the body and head of the
murdered Ethelbert, King of East Anglia, were brought to
Hereford for reburial, all previous attempts to inter the royal
remains having been frustrated by the appearance of
supernatural lights. At Hereford no strange lights appeared, but
water sprang from the ground where the king's body had been
temporarily put down.

Kentchurch   Kentchurch is said by some to have been the home
of the famous wizard Jack O'Kent. (See also **Grosmont** and
Trelleck, Gwent.) He is supposed to have occupied a bedroom in
Kentchurch Court and to have stabled his magic horses in the
Court's cellars. These horses could travel so swiftly that Jack was
able to take to London a pie cooked in the early morning in
Kentchurch, getting it to the capital in time for the English king's
breakfast.

Kidderminster   Here, in the middle of the nineteenth century,
lived the celebrated 'white witch' Becky Swan. Becky came to a
mysterious end: she is said to have admitted a large, strange,
black cat to her cottage, and to have lived with it for some days.
At the end of that time, neighbours who broke in found that
Becky had been reduced to a pile of ashes lying harmlessly on the
floor. The cat vanished up the chimney and was never seen
again.

Kington   Thomas, or 'Black', Vaughan was the bane of this
district in the middle decades of the fifteenth century, and his
wife ('Gethen the Terrible') was equally feared. After Vaughan
was killed at the Battle of Banbury in 1469, his malevolent spirit
continued to inflict harm on the district until a hard-drinking

priest managed to reduce it and imprison it in a snuff box, which was then thrown into Hergest Pool. Effigies of Thomas and Gethen can be seen in the Vaughan chapel in Kington Church.

Lickey Hills   The Devil is supposed to have hunted wild boars during the hours of darkness on the Lickey Hills. He is thought to have stabled his satanic hounds in Halesowen.

Malvern Hills   Raggedstone Hill – one of the Malvern Hills – is supposed to bring bad luck to anyone rash enough to stand in its shadow. The curse is said to have originated in the Middle Ages, when a monk from one of the Malvern priories was required, as a penance, to climb up Raggedstone Hill daily on his hands and knees. Looking down from the top, he would have seen those who had sent him up standing below, in the shade.

Marden   The present church at Marden is built on ground in which the murdered King Ethelbert was once temporarily interred. (See **Hereford**, **Herefordshire and Worcestershire**, above.) When Ethelbert's body was removed and taken to Hereford, water sprang mysteriously from the empty grave. 'St Ethelbert's Well', inside Marden Church, has been of interest to pilgrims for centuries.

Ross-on-Wye   The River Wye, near here, was for many years believed to be haunted by a female spectre sailing in a phantom boat. She would appear, usually, in the late evening, and would seem to be in great distress.

Sutton St Nicholas   The Wergin Stones, about a mile from the village, are said to have been moved from their original (and present) site by the Devil, in the middle of the seventeenth century. Nine yoke of oxen were needed to drag them back.

Weston Penyard   There is said to be treasure hidden in a cave or tunnel under the ruins of Penyard Castle. It is guarded – as in so many instances of such hoards – by a fierce and wakeful bird.

Worcester Several churches in the English and Welsh shires contain carved images of the Green Man, or 'Jack in the Green'. He was a pagan nature spirit, shown usually as a human face surrounded by branches and leaves, and his main job was to restore warmth and life to the earth each spring. A carving in the Cathedral cloisters, close to the Chapter House door, shows him with unusual clarity.

Further reading
Grice, Frederick, *Folk Tales of the West Midlands*, Thomas Nelson, 1952.
Merrill, John, *Legends and Folklore (The Midlands)*, Wayland, 1974.

Further information from
The County Librarian, County Library Headquarters, Love's Grove, Castle Street, Worcester, WR1 3BY.

Hertfordshire

Albury Halls Garden Pond, near the church, has for ages been said to be bottomless, and a hiding-place of the Devil.

Aldbury A medieval castle, here, is said to have been the home of a Sir Guy de Gravade, who made magical experiments. The castle vanished suddenly during the fourteenth century – as a result, possibly, of some experiments that had been a little too effective – but it is believed to reappear from time to time, on dark nights, with light streaming from its windows.

Berkhamsted St John's Well is believed to be fed by a spring credited since pre-Christian times with mysterious healing powers.

Brent Pelham   St Mary's Church contains, in its north wall, a puzzling tomb. Local traditions say that it contains the abnormally large bones of Piers Shonks, Lord of the Manor in the eleventh century. According to the most remarkable accounts of his end, Shonks managed to kill a particularly terrifying dragon that had been ravaging the district. When the Devil appeared, seeking revenge for the slaughter of his servant, and claimed Shonks, body and soul, Shonks shot an arrow to show where he wished to be buried safely, 'as in a fortress'. Where it landed, Shonks' tomb was built.

Burnham Green   Battles in pre-Norman times may be recalled by stories of ghostly white horses seen galloping at night round this district.

Codicote   The mediaeval woodcarving known as 'The Old Dog' in the parish church is said to bring good luck to those bold enough to pat it.

Datchworth   Near the old road from Bramfield, a disused chalk pit called 'Sally Rainbow's Dell' was once the home of a greatly feared witch.

Hitchin   The Offley Morris Men noted in this area have followed a long sequence of similar performers originating, probably, in pre-Christian times.

   The grounds of Hitchin Priory are said to be haunted, each June, by the ghost of a Cavalier who tried, vainly, to hide here, but was found by his enemies and killed at High Down House, close by.

Ippollitts   This place has associations with St Hippolytus, who may (or may not) have been buried here. It was famous at one time as a centre for the treatment of sick and injured horses, which are said to have derived great benefit from being brought to the saint's supposed shrine.

Knebworth   The ghost of a 'shining boy' seen at Knebworth House is supposed to have acted as a death warning to members of the Lytton family.

Markyate   The mansion Markyate Cell was the home in the seventeenth century of the spirited Lady Catherine Ferrers who, from a need for excitement, robbed travellers on the neighbouring highways. Her ghost – mounted, usually, on a large black horse – is said to have disturbed the country around, at times, since she was fatally wounded while holding up a coach near St Albans.

Preston   The ruins of Minsden Chapel, once said to be haunted by the spectre of a monk, have been more certainly haunted by hoaxers.

Royston   The hallowed 'Guardian Stone' near Royston Cross was for centuries supposed to keep the town safe from disaster.

Sawbridgeworth   The ghost of the eccentric Sir John Jocelyn, who died in 1741, is said to gallop occasionally on his grey hunter towards his old home at Hyde Hall.

St Albans   The name of St Alban, martyred on a hill near the town, recalls old stories of a stream that dried up when the condemned man approached, and reappeared, on higher ground, when he asked for water.

In more recent centuries, St Albans has been noted for its witches – in particular, a 'Mother Haggy', who was reputed to ride round on a traditional broomstick – and for its ghosts. There are said to be phantom monks in the precincts of the Abbey, and ghostly armies are said to clash in the district, recalling the battle fought in the Wars of the Roses.

Stevenage   Six barrows near the town are said to have been raised by the Devil.

St Paul's Walden   It is believed locally that the church should have been built near the 'bury', or manor house. Instead, the stones and other materials were transported magically, by night, to the church's present site.

Watford   The ghost of Lord Capel (1631–83) is said to reappear at his home, Cassiobury Park, on the anniversary of his death.

Wiggington   A phantom army is said to have been seen, and heard, here.

Further reading
Jones-Baker, Doris, *The Folklore of Hertfordshire*, Batsford, 1977.

Further information from
The Hertfordshire Local Studies Librarian, County Hall, Hertford, SG13 8EJ.

Humberside

Atwick   A ghostly highwayman has been seen here on numerous occasions. He is usually described as being headless.

Bridlington   In the town's Augustinian Priory, in the fourteenth century, lived and prayed a particularly holy man called St John. He is supposed to have had remarkable healing powers, and even to have brought some dead people back to life.

Burton Agnes   Burton Agnes Hall was built by three sisters in the early seventeenth century. The youngest sister – Anne Griffith – was attacked and mortally wounded by an outlaw. Before she died, she asked that her head should be preserved in her new home, which she so much admired. Her sisters ignored this request, and had her whole body buried in the local churchyard. Anne's unquiet spirit then started to haunt the Hall, causing so much disorder that her cadaver had to be disinterred and the skull brought indoors. It is kept now in a concealed niche in one of the walls.

Epworth   During part of the early eighteenth century the Rectory was the home of the Rev. Samuel Wesley, and members of his family. The Wesleys experienced a series of puzzling screams, bangings and other mysterious noises, and some members of the family were convinced that they could see the ghost that was causing the uproar.

Flamborough   The ghosts of a lady in white; of a headless woman; and of a girl called 'Jenny Gallows' are said to have been seen in the neighbourhood.

Harpham   A well near the church here is said to have given out ghostly drumming sounds whenever a member of the local landowning family, the St Quintons, was about to die. According to a story repeated for centuries in the district, a Norman St Quinton murdered a drummer boy and threw the lad's body into the well. The killing was seen by a witch who lived nearby, and she promptly put a spell on the family.

Haxey   Pagan rites associated with the winter solstice are thought to have been the precursors of the intriguing Hood Game, played here early in January during many centuries. As with Mumming Plays, these rites were intended to celebrate the triumph of light over darkness.

Pocklington   The Feathers Inn is said to be haunted by the ghost of a highwayman who was hanged in the inn's yard nearly two hundred years ago. He had murdered, in a particularly brutal fashion, a servant girl from the Feathers.

Rudston A standing stone in the churchyard here is said to be one of the tallest in this country. Local people say that it was thrown at the church by the Devil. His aim was not too sure, though – which accounts for its present position.

Watton Fields near the village are said to be visited by the headless nun Elfrida. She was an attractive young novice at Watton Abbey who fell in love with a local youth and left the community to live with him. When he learned that she was pregnant, he refused to have anything more to do with her. She is said to have returned to the Abbey, and to have pleaded for forgiveness. Her sins were too great for that, and she was beheaded.

Further information from
The Director of Leisure Services, Central Library, Albion Street, Hull, HU1 3TF.

Isle of Man

Ballona Bridge This has been known as 'The Fairy Bridge' because it has long been believed to be the home of supernatural beings. Some cautious Manx people still call out greetings to the Wee Folk as they cross the bridge.

Castletown The remains of Castle Rushen have, beneath them, an underground maze – or so it has been said. In the maze a giant is believed to lurk.

Glen Roy Nikkesen's Pool is said to be the home of a handsome young male water spirit. He is supposed to emerge occasionally from its depths. He is looking for a suitable girl to take down into the water, to keep him company.

Peel   The ruined castle here used to be haunted by a phantom hound known as 'The Moddey Dhoo', or 'Black Dog'. It was supposed to be harmless, as long as humans did not become too inquisitive about it.

Further reading
Killip, Margaret, *Folk-Lore of the Isle of Man*, Batsford, 1986.

Further information from
The Librarian, Town Hall, Douglas.

Isle of Wight

Chillerton   Charles I is believed to have escaped from Carisbrooke Castle and to have reached Billingham Manor, near here, in safety. The manor is said to have been haunted, since, by the ghost of the unfortunate king.

Gatcombe   A carved oak figure in Gatcombe Church is said to represent Edward Estur, who went crusading to the Holy Land in 1364, taking his mistress – one 'Lucy Lightfoot' – with him. Romantic tales about a nineteenth-century girl, also called Lucy Lightfoot, who fell passionately in love with the wooden effigy and who inexplicably vanished for ever when it was damaged during a great storm have little, if any, historical foundation.

Godshill   The church here was supposed to stand on a level place a little to the south-west of its present site, but the materials are said to have been moved by supernatural hands to a position that the owner of the hands preferred.

Knighton   The manor house at Knighton used to be known as 'Knighton Gorges' after one Ralph de Gorges married the daughter of the house. The mansion, one of the most impressive on the Isle of Wight, was demolished in 1820, and only the gateposts were left standing, but the sounds of music and laughter are still said to be heard, late at night, on occasions, such as New Year's Eve, when, in the old days, grand parties would have been held here.

Mottistone   This place is believed to have acquired its name from the thirteen-foot-high 'Long Stone' on the nearby hill. There have been suggestions that this may have been the 'meeting stone' of the Druids, and that on the sandstone pillar resting on the ground at its base they sacrificed white bulls to their god or gods.

St Helens   The successive churches here, being conspicuous, have made valuable landmarks for shipping. Men brought from the mainland to whitewash an earlier church found a wizened old man in old-fashioned clothes asleep on top of the tower. As he woke, they made fun of him. He told them that he remembered the men from the mainland who had built the church, some two hundred years before. They had been drowned on their return journey to Portsmouth, he told them, and that would be the fate, too, of the last men to touch the place. Dismissing the old stranger as a harmless eccentric, they got on with their task. When they packed up at the end of the day, the old man had vanished. His prophecy came true, however – the workmen's boat vanished on its way back to Portsmouth, and they were never seen again.

Further reading
Boase, Wendy, *The Folklore of Hampshire and the Isle of Wight*, Batsford, 1976.
Elder, Abraham, *Tales and Legends of the Isle of Wight*, 1839.

Further information from
The Assistant County Reference Librarian, Lord Louis Library, Orchard Street, Newport, Isle of Wight, PO30 1LL.

Kent

Ashford   At Eastwell Park, near here, a ghostly horseman is said to ride on every Midsummer Eve from the Pilgrims' Way, through the house, and into the lake. In some versions of the story, the rider is headless.

Aylesford   The megalithic burial chamber known as 'Kits Coty House' on Bluebell Hill is reputed to be the grave of a British chieftain, Catigern, who died fighting a Jutish invader, possibly Horsa, in AD 455. Their struggle is said to be fought again, from time to time, in silence, by ghostly figures. The jumbled stones not far away, known as 'Little Kits Coty House', are said to be impossible to count, because the Devil interferes with human attempts to do so.

Boughton Malherbe   The ghost of a monk dressed in grey is said to haunt the old rectory.

Canterbury   The paved passage known as 'The Dark Entry' between the Cathedral's Green Court and the old Infirmary Cloister is said to be haunted by the ghost of one Nell Cook. The woman, servant to one of the canons of the Cathedral, is said to have served a poisoned pie to her master and his niece, who, Nell Cook suspected, was also the Canon's mistress. According to the uncorroborated story, the ecclesiastical authorities had Nell Cook buried alive here, beneath the paving stones.

Cranbrook   The Church has tenuous associations with one 'Bloody Baker', possibly Sir Richard Baker, a reputed mass-murderer of Tudor times whose guilt was said to have been proved by the mysterious bloodstains on his gloves.

Downe   Two rooms in Downe Court are said to harbour atmospheres of evil – due, possibly, to Black Magic rituals once practised in them.

Faversham   The ghost of a Victorian seafaring man who died of exhaustion and exposure when refused admission to the inn is said to haunt the ancient Shipwrights Arms at Hollowshore. His reappearance is reputedly accompanied by an icy stream of air and a smell that is undefinable but unpleasant.

Goodwin Sands   These treacherous sandbanks off Deal have caused so many wrecks that it is almost inevitable that tales abound of phantom vessels seen in the vicinity. Best known, perhaps, are reports of the spectral three-masted schooner, the 'Lady Lovibond', that seems to reappear with predictable regularity at intervals of half a century.

Goudhurst   A house here is said to have suffered visits from apparitions of a malevolent type.

Harbledown   A well here, known as 'The Black Prince's Well', is reputed to have provided waters, hopefully with healing powers, for that prince. He is believed to have suffered from syphilis.

Hollingbourne   The ghost of Catherine Howard is said to have troubled those living in the Manor.

Isle of Thanet   The 'Hooden Horse' has traditionally appeared in these parts at some Midsummer and Christmastide festivities. It is a horse-head effigy, with a movable lower jaw, and may be a reminder of the pre-Christian worship, in the locality, of the Germanic god Woden. (In Norse, 'Odin'.) Woden, or Odin, god of wisdom and magic, was believed to ride a massive white stallion with eight hooves.

Kemsing   St Edith's Well is reputed to have had healing powers.

Lympne   The Castle is said to have a 'flying ghost' and other spectres.

Maidstone   The town is reputed to have been, once, a centre of witchcraft.

Minster-in-Sheppey   The tomb of Sir Robert de Shurland in the old monastic church has, behind the effigy of the knight, the head of a horse rising from some waves. This is supposed to represent the steed on which Sir Robert, escaping from justice, magically travelled two miles out to sea to seek the help of his Sovereign, Edward I. When, spared from the threat of death, Sir Robert returned to shore, he was told by a local witch that the horse, having saved his life, would later cause his death. He died, eventually, from the effects of a wound caused by a splinter from the horse's skull. There are other versions of this story.

Otford   A well in Otford is said to have been brought into being by Thomas à Becket. The ill-fated Archbishop, not thinking much of Otford's water, reputedly smote the ground with his crook. This ensured a purer supply.

Plaxtol   Old Soar Manor is said to be haunted by the ghost of a seventeenth-century dairymaid who committed suicide in the chapel.

Pluckley   This is sometimes said to be more haunted than any other town or village in Kent.

Rainham   A spectral coach is supposed to be driven from the church, which it leaves at midnight on Christmas Eve. It finishes its journey in the grounds of the house once occupied by Christopher Bloor, alive in the days of the Tudors. Presumably the headless passenger in the coach is the wraith of the late lamented Bloor.

Reculver   The walls of the Roman fort are haunted by the souls of the infants mercilessly sacrificed there, or so it is said. On tempestuous nights the little victims' cries can still be heard on the wind.

Rochester   Ghosts are said to have been seen at the Coopers' Arms, and other places in this old city.

Sissinghurst A staircase in the Castle is said to be haunted. It is known that the Castle was built by Sir Richard ('Bloody') Baker – the autocrat associated, too, with the church at **Cranbrook** (q.v.).

Strood Men of this place are believed to have cut off the tail of the sumpter-mule belonging to Thomas à Becket as the Archbishop passed through. For this, the descendants of the disrespectful men were condemned by Becket to be born with tails.

Trottiscliffe A 'Great Dogg' approached two packmen on the Pilgrims' Way near Trottiscliffe in 1745 and savaged and killed one of them. A ghostly hound, also threatening, has been seen more recently on this ancient track.

Tunbridge Wells The spa waters – tinged with red, and tasting of sulphur – are said to have been used by the Devil for cooling his nose after it had been pinched in a pair of red hot tongs by St Dunstan. (See **Mayfield, East Sussex**.)

Further reading
Dyer, B. R., *Kent Witches*, J. Pike, 1977.
Underwood, P., *Ghosts of Kent*, Meresborough Books, 1984.
Weaver, G., *Kent Ghosts*, J. Pike, 1977.

Further information from
The Local History Librarian, c/o The County Librarian,
    Springfield, Maidstone, ME14 2LH.

Lancashire

Ashton The hand of Father Edmund Arrowsmith, S.J., executed in 1628 for being a Romish priest, has been kept here for many years by the parish authorities. The relic is said to have had miraculous powers of healing.

Bacup   An unusual dance has traditionally been performed in the town at Easter. The team of eight dancers blacken their faces – presumably following the pagan belief that the magical effect of such rituals would be lessened if those who took part in them were recognised.

Black Rock   This small island in the estuary of the Mersey is said to have been, during the eighteenth century, the haunt of a mermaid. She was wooed by a local sailor, and gave him her ring as a token of affection, but a few days afterwards he died.

Burnley   At the Eagle's Crag, in Cliviger Gorge, a witch named Lady Sybil Towneley is said to have been buried by her husband, who had tried in vain to persuade her to give up her magical practices. Their ghosts are said to be visible at Hallowe'en.

Clitheroe   The stepping stones in the River Ribble at Brungerley, near here, are still said to be haunted by a malevolent sprite who claims at least one life every seven years. Unwary pedestrians using the stones are in danger of being swept off them by the sprite and consigned to a watery grave, or so local people believe.

Cockerham   The Devil is said once to have chosen Cockerham as his home, but the local people, alarmed at the new arrival, appointed the village schoolmaster to deal with the situation. Having met the Devil, the schoolmaster set him three tasks. The first two, the Devil accomplished easily. The third – the Fiend was required to make a rope of sand which could be washed in the River Cocker without losing a strand – was more than even the Devil could manage, and this drove him away.

Colne   The ruins of Wycoller Hall, near here, were said to be visited annually by a ghostly horseman – the spectre, it was believed, of a former inhabitant of the Hall who had murdered his wife in one of its rooms.

Garstang A bridge near here is reputed to be haunted by a 'boggart', or ghost of a woman murdered on or near the bridge.

Higher Penwortham Old tales linger of 'fairies' funerals' seen in the district.

Hoghton Here, fairies were said to live in the local rabbit burrows.

Lancaster In August 1612, ten witches were publicly hanged on a gallows a little way outside the boundaries of the city. All but one of them came from the remote Pendle Forest, and all but one of them – Alice Nutter, of Roughlee Hall – were poor. Some were so old and worn that it is a wonder that they had survived their pre-trial imprisonment. The evidence on which the accused were convicted seems, today, virtually incredible.

Leyland This is another English town with a 'church is in the wrong spot' tradition. At Leyland, the church is supposed to have been moved by magical means to its present site, having, originally, been completed some distance away.

Longridge Lanes and roads in the district around this small town were said to be haunted, centuries ago, by the ghost of a headless woman. The spectre had an unpleasant habit of chasing travellers to whom she took exception.

Newchurch A carved stone boss on the tower of the church in this Pendle Forest village is believed to symbolise the Eye of God. It may have been put there to protect the local people from the Devil, or from the witches who were later to give the district a reputation for evil.

Preston This is one of several towns in Lancashire at which 'egg-rolling' and other ceremonies involving eggs have been annually observed, at Easter.

Walk Mill   The Barcrofts lived at Barcroft Hall, near here, for many generations. Then (it is said) one of the heirs to Barcroft was some kind of idiot. Eventually, he was chained up in one of the cellars by a younger brother and starved to death. During one of his lucid moments, the prisoner pronounced a curse on the Barcroft family, willing that the name should perish for ever, and that the property should pass into other hands. He left some frenzied scribblings on the cellar wall, too, which are still there.

Further reading

Harland, J., and Wilkinson, T. T., *Lancashire Legends*, George Routledge & Sons, London, 1873; E.P. Publishing Limited, Wakefield, 1973 (reprint).

Harland, J., and Wilkinson, T. T., *Lancashire Folk-Lore*, John Heywood, Manchester and London, 1882; S.R. Publishers Limited, 1972 and E.P. Publishing Limited, 1973 (reprint).

Further information from

The Local Studies Librarian, County Library Headquarters, 143 Corporation Street, Preston, PR1 2TB.

Leicestershire

Belvoir   Early in the seventeenth century the Earl and Countess of Rutland, who lived in Belvoir Castle, incurred the displeasure of a local witch, one Joan Flower. Two of Joan Flower's daughters were in service at the Castle, but one of them – Margaret – was accused of theft and was dismissed. With her daughters and three other women, Joan Flower then set out to get her revenge. In less than a year, both of the Earl's young sons were dead. (Their effigies can be seen in the church at Bottesford. The inscription tells that they 'dyed in their infancy by wicked practice and sorcerye'.) At their trial in Lincoln, Joan Flower and her associates admitted that they had caused the deaths of the children by 'enchantments'. Joan Flower attempted momentarily to evade the consequences of her wicked deeds by withdrawing her confession, but when she asked for bread, saying 'May this choke me if I am guilty', it did exactly that. The other members of the Flower coven were hanged at Lincoln on 11 March 1618.

Bottesford   In the church here is the tomb of the 6th Earl of Rutland, reputed to have been made sterile by witchcraft. On the tomb are the effigies of his two sons mentioned above (see **Belvoir**).

Bradgate   When she was a child, the unfortunate Lady Jane Grey lived in the big house in Bradgate Park. Since she was executed in the Tower of London in 1553, her ghost has been said to haunt the Park, being seen or heard, usually, around Christmas.

Braunston   By the north wall of the church there is a strange figure carved from stone, and very obviously female. It is believed to represent an 'earth mother' of some kind, and may have been the centre of fertility-bringing ceremonies carried out here long before the church was built.

Edmundthorpe   Buried in St Michael's Church here is Sir Roger Smith, who died in the seventeenth century. With him are his two wives – both shown as effigies on the Smith tomb. The effigy that represents Lady Ann has on one wrist a noticeable stain. This is supposed to remind those who see it of an unfortunate injury caused when Lady Ann changed herself, by magic, into a cat. Her manservant, alarmed and disapproving, picked up a meat cleaver and hit the beast.

Griffydam   There is an old well here that is said to have been jealously guarded, long ago, by a fearsome beast known as a griffin. The griffin refused to let the villagers draw water from the well and they were forced to fetch all they needed from another source, two miles away. The griffin was seen eventually by a knight who happened to be passing by and who took pity on the villagers. Calling for a bow and arrows, he put an end to the nuisance.

Hallaton   Games held here at Easter are usually believed to have originated in pre-Christian days, though more recently they have been enjoyed under the auspices of the local church. Contests between teams from Hallaton and a neighbouring parish may be tenuous reminders of ancient rituals in which the spirits of winter would be overcome by those of spring.

Husbands Bosworth   The handsome mansion Bosworth Hall (sometimes now referred to as 'Bosworth Park') has, on a ceiling, a dark stain which takes the shape, more or less, of a woman's hand. The stain, it is said, cannot be hidden, however many times it is painted over, and it recalls the dreadful fate of Anna Dixie, daughter of Sir Wolston Dixie, the fourth Baronet, who owned the Hall a little more than two centuries ago. The story goes that Sir Wolston found out that his daughter was secretly meeting one of the workers on his estate. The Baronet, disapproving of her association with a social inferior, forbade her to see him any more. To augment this prohibition, he arranged for a mantrap of some kind to be set near the couple's trysting place. Unfortunately for the father, the girl disobeyed him and reached the rendezvous before the young man did. Dreadfully wounded, she was carried back to the Hall, where she lay bleeding until she died, a few days later.

The ghost of Anna Dixie is not the only one said to haunt Bosworth Hall – the mansion is also haunted by the ghost of the Protestant Lady Lisgar, who lived there towards the end of the nineteenth century. Her restlessness is said to have been caused by the obduracy she showed during her lifetime: when one of the old Catholic servants in the Hall was dying, Lady Lisgar is alleged to have refused to let a priest enter the house to administer the last rites. For this, the lady is said to be doomed to wander along the passages and up and down the stairways of the Hall into the foreseeable future.

Leicester   This large industrial city was once a relatively small settlement, dominated by the terrifying hag Black Annis, who lay in wait on the nearby Dane Hills, hoping to catch any disobedient children who might wander away from their homes. 'Annis' may well have been a corrupted form of 'Anu'. Anu was the wife of the Celtic Lud, god of the heavens.

Oakham   A fine collection of horseshoes, bringers of luck, belongs to the Lord of the Manor. It is believed that Elizabeth I donated the original shoe in 1600. Since then, every member of the Royal Family or peer visiting Rutland has been expected to make a contribution.

Wistow   The lonely church of St Wistan, here, recalls the young Saxon prince Wistan, who should have inherited the throne of Mercia. Wistan got into trouble with his kinsman Britfardus, though, when Britfardus wanted to marry Wistan's mother and Wistan opposed the alliance. Britfardus invited Wistan to this deserted place to talk over the difficulties that had arisen between them. Here, the older man murdered the prince and buried his body. The foul deed could not be concealed – strange lights appeared over the place where the body lay, and human hairs started to grow out of the ground. Though the saint's bones have long ago been taken away, the incriminating hairs are said to reappear each year at Wistow on the first day of June, the anniversary of the assassination.

Further reading
Cutting, Angela, *Leicestershire Ghost Stories*, Anderson, 1982.
Green, Susan E., *Selected Legends of Leicester*, The Information
    Bureau, Bishop Street, Leicester.

Further information from
The Leicestershire Studies Librarian, Information Centre, Bishop
    Street, Leicester, LE1 6AA.

Lincolnshire

Anwick Two big stones by the entrance to the churchyard are said to have guardian spirits which visibly take the forms, occasionally, of a pair of drakes.

Bardney The remains of St Oswald, kept in Bardney Abbey in early Christian times, were believed to have miraculous healing powers.

Caistor A big stone on Fonaby Top is said to have been, some twelve centuries ago, a sack of seed corn. A holy man, passing by, asked the farmer who tilled the land there to give him some corn to feed his ass. The farmer alleged that he had no corn. The holy man pointed to the sack. 'That is a stone, not a sack', countered the farmer. To teach the farmer a lesson, the holy man made sure that the sack really did become a stone. To this day, bad luck is said to come to anyone who interferes with the petrified sack.

Cranwell The Newark to Sleaford road (A17) crosses the ancient Ermine Street (Leicester to Lincoln) at a spot known as 'Bayard's Leap'. Bayard was a blind horse said to have been selected by magical means for the hazardous task of carrying away a local witch who was the terror of the neighbourhood. The witch struggled fiercely, wounding the horse so grievously with her talons that it leaped sixty feet. Iron horseshoes mark the place (approximately) where this great jump happened.

Fishtoft The local church is dedicated to the seventh-century Saint Guthlac. Guthlac is shown in a window of the church holding a whip, said to have been given to him by St Bartholomew. While the saint held the whip, local traditions recall, the town would not be troubled by rats or other small vermin.

Glentham A Lady Tournay, who died in the fourteenth century, is commemorated by a stone figure in Glentham Church. Until the reign of William IV, the effigy was carefully scrubbed, before each Easter, by seven old spinsters. The washers were rewarded with money collected as rent for some land that had been bequeathed for the purpose.

Holbeach The Chequers Inn is said to have been particularly favoured, in the olden days, by card-playing customers. Ghosts of some of the keenest of these addicts are said to reappear from time to time in the local church, where, in life, they played a 'last rubber' with one of their usual associates who had expired.

Lincoln Tales of human sacrifices, of blood-collecting for the purposes of sorcery, and of other malpractices were freely used to bring discredit on Jewish people in England in the twelfth century. Lincoln was the scene of one of the most lurid of all anti-Semitic campaigns, when the Jews of the city were accused of stealing a boy of eight or nine years old, whose name was Hugh, and of scourging, crucifying and disembowelling him. Three of the oldest houses in Britain can still be visited in Lincoln. Their names – the Jew's House and Jews' Court in the Strait and Aaron the Jew's House on Steep Hill – evoke memories of the furore over little St Hugh.

Louth The land around Thorpe Hall is said to have been haunted for nearly four centuries by a ghostly Spanish lady, dressed in green. She is supposed to have been captured in her own country by a former owner of the Hall, who refused to bring her back to England because he was already happily married. The Spanish lady, who had fallen in love with her captor, was displeased.

Skegness A footpath near Gunby Hall, a little to the west of Skegness, is said to be haunted by the ghosts of a handsome manservant and of young Margaret Massingberd who, in the late seventeenth century, fell in love with him. Margaret's father, incensed by his daughter's disregard of the social proprieties, shot the man dead as the pair tried to elope.

Further reading
Gutch and Peacock, *County Folklore, Volume 5 (Lincolnshire)*, The Folklore Society, 1908.
Rudkin, E., *Lincolnshire Folklore*, Beltons, 1936.

Further information from
The Reference Librarian, Central Reference Library, Freeschool Lane, Lincoln, LN2 1EZ.

Norfolk

Aylmerton Circular hollows near here are believed to have been in existence since the Stone Age – they may have been parts of human dwellings or they may have been used for the excavation of flints. Whatever their purpose, they seem to have been associated with great sadness, for the ghostly figure of a distressed woman in white has been several times reported from the neighbourhood of the pits, and loud screams have frequently been heard.

Bawburgh Water from St Walstan's Well, near the church, was used for centuries for treating the illnesses and injuries of animals.

Blickling The Hall at Blickling has taken the place of an even older house in which Anne Boleyn was born. The ghost of Henry VIII's ill-fated Queen is believed, now, to haunt the Hall and its surroundings, appearing as if by prior appointment at midnight on each 19 May, the anniversary of her execution. The ghost of her father, Sir Thomas Boleyn, is thought to range widely over the land round Blickling.

Castle Rising   Silence in the Norman keep here is said to be broken occasionally by heartrending cries. These are believed to come from the unhappy shade of Queen Isabella, widow of Edward II. The Queen was imprisoned in these grim walls after she had agreed to the murder of her husband in Berkeley Castle.

East Dereham   A well near the church is associated with St Withburga, who founded a religious house in the locality during the seventh century. At a time when food was scarce, she is believed to have induced by prayer two deer to provide milk for her nuns.

East Raynham   The Hall at East Raynham has reputedly been haunted for many years by the ghost of a tall lady dressed in brown. The appearance of this female is made more frightening by the fact that she has no eyes, but empty sockets only.

Great Melton   A ghostly coach with horses driven by a headless coachman is said to have been seen on the Old Norwich Road. The passengers in the coach appear to have been the ghosts of four young bridesmaids who were killed by a highwayman when they were returning home from a wedding. The girls' deaths were assumed to be accidental until repeated sightings of the spectral coach convinced the local authorities that dirty work had been done.

Griston   Wayland Wood, near here, is believed to be haunted by the ghosts of two children who, by orders of their wicked uncle and guardian, were taken into it and left to starve.

Happisburgh   The coast near here was frequented, at one time, by many smugglers. After a quarrel between some of them over the division of their spoil, there was a killing. The ghost of a dreadfully maimed man was frequently seen after that at the scene of the crime.

Horning   The ruins of the Abbey of St Benet's Hume have been painted by many artists. A fearsome winged dragon once made its lair in the vaults of the Abbey, or so local people have believed. The Old Ferry Inn, not far from the Abbey, is said to be haunted by the green-clad ghost of a girl. This restless spirit is thought to have been, long ago, a girl who was raped by drunken monks from the Abbey. They are said to have killed the girl after they had finished with her and to have thrown her body into the river, hoping that their misdeeds would not be discovered.

Potter Heigham   Several ghosts have reputedly been seen or heard in this neighbourhood. The most audible is almost certainly the spectral drummer, dressed in military fashion, who is said to skate on wintry nights across Hickling Broad, recalling a real-life drummer boy who perished here in the early nineteenth century when attempting to cross the ice to meet his sweetheart. The ghost of an eighteenth-century Lady Carew, too, is said to be seen by the River Thurne. That unfortunate lady is believed, like so many others, to have sold her soul to the Devil. She disappeared into the waters of the Thurne on her wedding night, after the Devil's envoys had arrived in a ghostly carriage to take her away.

Thetford   Here, too, there have been reports of several ghosts – at the Bell Inn, where the spectre is said to be that of a former landlady who was murdered by her lover; near Thetford Warren, where the wraith appears to be suffering most wretchedly from leprosy; and there are other, less well-authenticated local revenants.

Tunstall   The church bells of Tunstall are said to have been stolen, long ago, by the Devil. The foul fiend is believed to have taken them underground, from where their tolling can sometimes be distinctly heard by those with well-tuned ears.

Walsingham   Here, in the eleventh century, the Virgin Mary is said to have appeared in a vision to the wife of a local nobleman. The place became, after that, a centre of pilgrimage, and travellers from many parts of Europe came to see the Walsingham Shrine and to sample the water from Our Lady's Well, which reputedly had extraordinary healing powers.

Waxham   Six members of the Brograve family, who lost their lives at various times in battle, are said to haunt Waxham Hall.

Further reading

Barrett, W. H., and Garrod, R. P., *East Anglian Folklore and Other Tales*, Routledge & Kegan Paul, 1976.

Crossley-Holland, Kevin, *The Dead Moon and Other Tales from East Anglia and the Fen Country*, Deutsch, 1982.

Dixon, G. M., *Folktales and Legends of Norfolk*, Minimax Books, 1980.

Further information from

The County Local Studies Librarian, Central Library, Bethel Street, Norwich, NR2 1NJ.

Northamptonshire

Abthorpe   The Manor House is reputedly visited by the ghost of a Franciscan friar.

Boughton   The ruined church is said to be haunted in mid-winter by the ghost of George Catherall, a local gang-leader who was hanged at Northampton in 1826.

Broughton   Each year, on the first Sunday after 12 November, the inhabitants of this attractive village have been accustomed to parade together, banging tin cans and other improvised 'instruments', and generally making as much noise as they possibly can. The parade, starting at the church gates at midnight, is thought to have originated in the Middle Ages, and its aim has been to frighten away gipsies, who, being especially superstitious, would not wish to stay in a place where strange quasi-magical rituals were publicly repeated.

Church Stowe St Michael's Church here is said to be built on a site selected by a sprite, described by a medieval historian as 'a creetur no bigger nor a hog'. Eight times, the builders of the church tried to raise its walls elsewhere. On each occasion, the sprite demolished their work and moved the materials and their tools to its preferred location. At last the builders gave up and accepted the 'creetur's' decision.

Clopton A man called 'Skulking Dudley' used to live in Clopton Manor in the fifteenth century, and made a great nuisance of himself in the district. Challenged to fight a duel by a neighbouring landowner whom he had insulted, Dudley pretended to be ill, and let his daughter put on his armour in his place. She fought the duel, and lost. Her adversary was about to kill her, but when he removed Dudley's helmet and saw the face of the girl inside it, he fell in love with her, and eventually they were married. Dudley, murdered by one of his agricultural workers whom he had grossly mistreated, went on haunting the district until his unquiet spirit was exorcised.

Daventry King Charles I is known to have stayed at the Wheatsheaf Hotel in Sheep Street in 1645. His army was encamped in the vicinity. During one night, he was visited by the ghost of his old friend and supporter Thomas Wentworth, Earl of Strafford, whom he had surrendered to Parliament in 1641, and who had subsequently been executed. Charles, who had been warned not to engage the Roundhead army in battle, was awakened from his sleep by the ghost, who urged him to ignore the warning. He would have been better off if he had heeded it, however, for on the following day he suffered a crushing defeat at the Battle of Naseby – a reverse from which he was fated never to recover.

Guilsborough Two local women – Agnes Browne and her daughter Jane – were executed here in 1616 after having been found guilty of causing the deaths of several young villagers by witchcraft. The Brownes were said to have travelled round the district on the back of a sow.

Ringstead A sad ghost that has haunted this district is believed to have been the shade of Lydia Astley, a young girl who went missing in 1850, after she had been spurned by the man she loved. The ghost's walk used to finish at a spot at which, in 1865, the skeleton of a girl was found, concealed in a ditch.

Weedon St Werburgha, patron saint of women and children, who lived in the seventh century, spent several years at Weedon Abbey. Here she is said to have performed several miracles, the most spectacular of them being the taming and domestication of a great gaggle of wild geese, which were causing havoc in the neighbourhood with their greedy ways.

Woodford In a pillar in the north arcade of Woodford Church there is a little window. Behind this window, there is a human heart. If the story told locally is correct, this is the heart of a Vicar of Woodford who was deprived of his living, shortly after the Reformation, on account of his Catholic beliefs. He took refuge in a religious house in Belgium where, shortly afterwards, he died. His heart was brought back to Woodford a few years later by a new Vicar, named Andrew Powlet. After Powlet himself died, the hiding-place of the heart of the previous incumbent was forgotten. It was only relocated when Powlet's ghost appeared in Woodford Rectory in 1862 and showed the young clergyman who then had the living where to search.

Further reading
Pipe, Marian, *Legends of Northamptonshire*, Nenarts, 1984.

Further information from
The District Librarian, The Central Library, Abington Street,
    Northampton, NN1 2BA.

Northumberland

Allendale The departure of each Old Year has been celebrated
here for centuries with ceremonies based on ancient fire rituals.
These were almost certainly pagan, and magical in their intent.

Alnwick A well in Alnwick Park has long been renowned for its
ability to make wishes come true. The suppliant is required to
drop at least one pin into the water before stating his or her
request.

Bamburgh Below the Castle, there is said to be a secret cave, the
doors of which swing open only once in each seven years, on
Christmas Eve. In the cave sits a toad, waiting to become, once
again, the Queen of Northumbria.
    The story is ancient, and it concerns a King of Northumbria
who remarried in his old age, not knowing that his bride was a
witch. The bride, jealous of the old King's daughter, turned the
princess by magic into a dragon known locally as the 'Laidley
Worm'. The Worm started to devastate the country round, and
went on doing so – as dragons were wont to do – until at last the
King's son, the Childe of Wynde, undertook to kill the monster.
Tethering his horse to the Spindlestone (an upright stone pillar
still to be seen near Bamburgh) he moved in to the attack without
realising that the creature was really his sister. The Worm
declined to do battle, and, instead, told the Childe of Wynde its
story. This was sufficient to reverse the magical process. The
Worm became once again a Princess, and the wicked Queen was
turned into a toad.

Bardon Mill A thief killed at Hardriding Farm, near here, in the fourteenth century, is said to have returned, in ghostly form, at intervals since.

Blanchland The Lord Crewe Arms Hotel is believed to have a female ghost. This may be the sister of the Jacobite General Thomas Forster, who went into exile in Europe after the Stuart cause was irretrievably lost. Forster is reputed to have hidden, at one time, in the hotel.

Broomlee Lough This lake is one of several in the British Isles reputed to contain King Arthur's magic sword Excalibur, surrendered as the king lay dying.

Callaly The castle at Callaly is said to have been partly built on the nearby hill. Each morning, the workmen found that the stones assembled on the previous day had been scattered, by supernatural means, during the hours of darkness. At last the hint was taken and Callaly Castle was put up on its present site.

Dilston The Castle is believed to be haunted by the ghost of the tragic widow of the last Earl of Derwentwater. The Earl was executed in London in 1716, after having supported the abortive Jacobite rising of the previous year. He had not intended to, but he was virtually compelled by the taunts of his wife to join the rebels.

Elsdon After eighteenth-century murderer William Winter's body was exhibited in a gibbet a little way to the south-east of Elsdon, sufferers from toothache used to cut slivers of wood from its grim timbers, believing that these, if rubbed on the painful gums, would give them relief.

Farne Islands The evil spirits that lived from time immemorial on and above the Farne Islands were banished – or so it is said – by St Cuthbert when he made his home here in the seventh century. Since then, they have been hovering on the periphery of the islands, where their screams of rage (or torment) can still occasionally be heard.

Featherstone The land round Featherstone Castle is said to be haunted by a number of ghosts. These may be the shades of those who attended a tragic wedding, a long time ago. As the members of the bridal party passed through Pinkingscleugh Glen, they are thought to have been attacked and murdered by a man that the bride had rejected.

Hedley-on-the-Hill The district round Hedley was for a long time plagued by a playful sprite or bogle known as the 'Hedley Kow'. The sprite would often take the form of a lively horse, and would conclude each of its pranks with a loud 'Ha! Ha!'

Horsley Nafferton Tower, by the Whittle Burn, is an unfinished peel tower. Here, according to legend, a man called 'Long Lonkin' or 'Long Lamkin' murdered a woman and her child. His ghost is believed to haunt the place.

Lindisfarne In the churchyard on Holy Island there is a stone known locally as the 'Petting Stone'. (In fact, it may well be part of the base of the cross of St Cuthbert, who lived here in the seventh century). Brides leaving the church after their weddings are usually advised to jump over the stone in the belief that doing so would help them to enter a new way of life.

Longwitton Three wells in the gardens of Longwitton Hall have been believed, for centuries, to have unusual healing powers.

Newbrough The remains of Old Meg – a witch burned alive in the sixteenth century – are said to have been buried by a stream about a mile north of Newbrough. As her blackened body was interred, a pointed stick was driven through her heart to prevent her spirit wandering.

Sewingshields   King Arthur and his knights are said to be sleeping in a cave somewhere beneath the ruins of Sewingshields Castle.

Stamfordham   Black Heddon, near here, used to be haunted by a boggart or playful spirit whose tricks were so frustrating that villagers were compelled to carry around sprigs of rowan, the traditional safeguard against witchcraft.

Wark   Three wells here used to be visited early on New Year's Day by those who wanted their most urgent wishes to come true. The journey used to become a race, as it was believed that the first drinker would have the greatest chance of success.

Whalton   The ancient pagan festival of bonfire-making on Midsummer's Eve has been continued here into the present decade.

Further reading
Richardson, M. A., *The Local Historian's Table Book of Remarkable Occurrences, Historical Facts, Traditions . . . etc., connected with the Counties of Newcastle-upon-Tyne, Northumberland and Durham*, M. A. Richardson, Newcastle-upon-Tyne, 1844.

Further information from
The County Librarian, The County Library, The Willows, Morpeth, Northumberland, NE61 1TA.

North Yorkshire

Aldborough   Three large standing stones between Aldborough and Boroughbridge are known locally as 'The Devil's Arrows'. They are supposed to have been aimed by the Devil at an early Christian community.

Appletreewick   The chasm known as 'Trollers Gill' has been thought, for centuries, to be haunted by trolls or ferocious phantom hounds. The body of a man found dead here in 1881 bore marks that could not have been made by mortal hands.

Askrigg   A female ghost dressed in garments of the Tudor age is said to haunt Nappa Hall.

Bedale   Snape Castle is said to be haunted by the ghost of Catherine Parr, last wife of Henry VIII.

Beningbrough   The banks of the River Ouse near here are said to be haunted by the ghost of a murdered woman. The woman was housekeeper to the family who lived in Beningbrough Hall during the late seventeenth century. Because she refused to allow the steward of the estate to seduce her, he paid a local poacher, William Vasey, to murder her. Vasey was caught and hanged at York.

Burnsall   Elbolton Hill, near here, has for many years been reputed to be a favourite haunt of fairies and other wee folk.

Farndale West   The mound near here known as 'Obtrush Tumulus' was believed, a century ago, to be the home of a frightening bogle or 'Hobthrush'.

Giggleswick   The waters of the Ebbing and Flowing Well here do exactly that, with great regularity. The well is said to be the home of a mysterious maiden. When she was being chased by a satyr, she called on the gods for help. They saved her by turning her into this spring. Its flow was – and presumably still is – activated by the frenzied beating of the frightened nymph's heart.

Goathland   This is one of several places in the north and east of England where sword-dance teams have regularly performed their ancient and mystical rituals, in the darkest weeks of the year.

Hutton-le-Hole   The Folk Museum here has acquired a number of 'witch-posts' – carved beams once intended to keep homesteads safe from invasion by witches.

Knaresborough   In a small cave here, in 1488, a female baby was born. Her mother died in giving birth to her, while mysterious noises echoed through the cave. The child, as she grew, soon showed that she was the mistress of supernatural powers, and that she had the gift of prophecy. In 1512 she married a man from Shipton, near York, and – known widely as 'Mother Shipton' – became the most notorious of all Yorkshire's many celebrated witches.

Nunnington   This place is said to have been plagued, during the Middle Ages, by a winged dragon with magical powers. The creature was finally attacked by a Peter Loschy, who fought with it for hours. Each time Loschy injured the beast it would roll over, and its wounds would instantly close. Loschy finally achieved victory over the beast by hacking off whole pieces of its flesh, which his hound would then carry away out of range of the beast's magical curing capacity. A stone effigy in the local church is said by some to represent the ingenious Peter Loschy.

Richmond   King Arthur and his knights are said to be temporarily asleep in a cavern reached by means of a secret passage under Richmond Castle. At least two intruders are believed to have entered this passage, or a related subterranean walkway. One – a drummer boy – was instructed to beat his drum as he went, so that his progress could be heard by his companions above ground. Before the boy had gone a mile, his drumming stopped, and that was the end of him. Ghostly echoes of his drumbeats can still be heard in the district on quiet nights, or so it is claimed.

Runswick   A small cave near Runswick Bay is still called the 'Hob Hole'. For centuries, it has been believed to be the home of a hob, boggart or troll. Having been told that such creatures are able to cure whooping cough, local parents whose children have been suffering from this ailment have taken the little patients along to the Hole. Once there, the parents have invoked the occupant's aid by reciting:

'Hob-Hole Hob!
My bairn's gettin' t' kink cough.
Tak' 't off! Tak' 't off!'

Saltergate   At the Saltergate Inn, high on the North Yorkshire moors, a peat fire has been kept burning for at least two hundred years, without being allowed to go out. According to a local tradition, the Devil or some other evil spirit is trapped beneath the hearth. Disaster will surely come to the Inn and those who live in and visit it, it is believed, if the peat stops smouldering.

Scarborough   Two ghosts are most often talked about in Scarborough – the black horse which is reputed to have haunted the town for almost eight hundred years; and the ghost of Lydia Bell, daughter of a well-known York confectioner. The girl was found strangled on Scarborough Beach in 1804.

Slingsby   The road that joins Hovingham and Malton has a distinct bend near Slingsby. Local people say that this deviation was made to avoid the lair of a serpent or dragon which used to live by preying on those who travelled on the road, while it was still straight. The serpent was eventually killed by a local landowner named Wyvill. Both Wyvill and his dog are believed to have perished after the fight, the venom they had inhaled having proved too much for them. An effigy of an unidentified knight in Slingsby Church has been said by some to represent an early Wyvill.

Spofforth   The tower, which is virtually all that remains of Spofforth Castle, is said to be haunted. The female ghost appears at the top of the tower. There it stands quite motionless for some moments. Then it appears to take a suicidal leap towards the ground below.

Summer Bridge Pagan rituals are supposed to have been observed at Brimham Rocks, still called by such names as 'Druid's Altar' and 'Druid's Head'.

Thorpe The bridge known as 'Dibble's Bridge' is supposed locally to have been built by the Devil. A shoemaker, wet after being compelled to swim through the flooded river, sat down on the riverbank to dry. As he waited, he sang. The Devil came, and started to sing the choruses. The two got on well together. At last, the shoemaker offered the Devil a drink. In return for the shoemaker's generosity, the Devil undertook to grant his companion one wish. The shoemaker asked for a bridge, to make the task of delivering his wares less hazardous. His wish was granted, and the bridge has been here ever since.

Threshfield A well here has been supposed for centuries to have miraculous or magical powers. Those frightened of witches, demons and other malicious beings have looked to the well for sanctuary.

Whitby The royal and saintly Hild founded Whitby Abbey more than thirteen hundred years ago. She is believed to have rid the whole of Eskdale of snakes by driving them over the edge of a cliff into the sea. Ammonite fossils – clearly resulting from Hild's zeal – are portrayed in the heraldic achievements of St Hilda's Colleges at Oxford and Durham.

York This ancient city is so well provided with ghosts that a book has been published that deals with this subject alone. (See **Further reading**, below). Among the best-known York phantoms are the ghost of Dean Gale, who died in the Minster in 1702, and has since been seen there, sitting in his favourite pew; spectral Roman soldiers seen at The Treasurer's House; a male ghost wearing a wide-brimmed hat seen at the Cock and Bottle Inn; the ghost of a nun seen in the Theatre Royal; and a phantom army seen at Stockton-in-the Forest, four miles from the city.

Further reading
Mitchell, J. V., *Ghosts of an Ancient City*, Ceralis Press, 1982.

Further information from
The Assistant County Librarian, North Yorkshire County Library Divisional Headquarters, Museum Street, York, YO1 2DS.
The Assistant County Librarian, North Yorkshire County Library Divisional Headquarters, 1 Thirsk Road, Northallerton, North Yorkshire, DL6 1PT.

Nottinghamshire

Blidworth Ancient 'plough plays' have been performed over the centuries here, and in several other Nottinghamshire villages and small towns (e.g. Bothamsall, Clayworth, East Bridgford, Flintham, Mansfield, North Leverton, Norwell, Selston, Tollerton, Walesby, Whatton and Worksop). In some places, the plays are no longer performed. In others, they have lapsed and have been occasionally revived. The plays would probably have been performed, in less sophisticated times, by teams of Plough Boys (or 'Jacks', 'Jags', 'Stots' or 'Bullocks': each team might inherit a variant name). On Plough Monday – usually the second Monday in January – the participants would place a light in the local church, and would then enact a traditional drama in which the names of the characters – 'Threshing Blade', 'Lady Bright and Gay', 'The Sergeant', 'Beelzebub', 'The Doctor', and so on – are many centuries old. At the climax of the play, Threshing Blade (or his equivalent) would be killed in a mock duel and afterwards would be brought back to life by the boastful Doctor. By the processes of sympathetic magic, certainly dating back to pre-Christian times, Threshing Blade would be representing the death of the earth in winter and its resurrection in spring, without which the spring ploughing, which began on or shortly after Plough Monday, would be a labour lost. After each performance of the play, the actors would beg for cash donations to supplement their meagre earnings, and might sing some folk tune, like this one recorded at Blidworth in 1925:

> Good Master and good Mistress,
>   As you sit round your fire,
> Have pity on us Plough Boys who plough
>   Through mud and mire.
> A pint of your best beer,
>   A pint of your best beer,
> We'll thank you for your kindnesses
>   And a pint of your best beer.

In return for alms and/or hospitality, some Plough Boys could be persuaded to do a little work on their benefactor's land, even if this was only token labour.

Harlow Wood   A stone on the roadside near here marks the spot on which an attractive seventeen-year-old girl called Bessie Shepherd was brutally beaten to death nearly two centuries ago. The Sheffield man who murdered her was caught in a Mansfield public house where he was trying to sell the shoes he had stolen from her, and was hanged, later, at Nottingham. Ever since then, the ghost of his young victim is said to have materialised on the Mansfield to Nottingham road whenever her stone memorial has been disturbed in any way.

Newark-on-Trent   A well in Devon Park is usually known as 'St Catherine's Well'. Here, two thirteenth-century knights, previously friendly, are said to have come to blows, their quarrel being caused by their mutual love for a lady called Isabell de Caldwell. As the victorious knight – one Sir Guy Saucimer – dashed away, leaving his rival dead on the ground, water gushed upwards, and went on flowing, cold and clear. But the story does not end there: Sir Guy, it is said, went abroad in an attempt to atone for his crime, and while he was overseas he contracted leprosy. (The Lady Isabell, predictably, was dying at home of a broken heart.) Urged by St Catherine, who appeared to him in a dream, Sir Guy came back to Newark-on-Trent, bathed in the waters of the mysterious well, and was cured of his leprosy. Gratefully, the knight built a hermitage by the well, and, with this as his centre, devoted the rest of his life sadly and soberly to religious ends. He is properly remembered now as 'St Guthred'.

Newstead The Abbey, built in the twelfth century, was for a long time the home of the Byron family. According to Washington Irving, who visited the place, the poet had had a notion that there was a lot of money buried about the Abbey by the monks, and in an attempt to find it he had the flagstones in the cloisters taken up. His workmen dug and dug, but found nothing but stone coffins filled with bones. Byron had one of the coffins placed in the Abbey's great hall; several of the skulls he had cleaned, for use as ornaments. The ghostly reputation that the place already had would have been undoubtedly enhanced by these macabre embellishments.

Many of the stories concerning ghosts at Newstead Abbey include the Woman in White, said to be the shade of Sophia Hyatt, a bookseller's daughter who was an ardent admirer of Byron. Her obsessive behaviour became noticeable in her lifetime. Since her death, it is claimed, she has haunted his old home, wildly calling out his name. Other stories feature a Black Friar, sometimes known as 'The Goblin'. The appearance of the Black Friar has usually been held to portend some evil threatening the master of the mansion. Byron claimed – or pretended – that he had seen it about a month before he contracted his ill-starred marriage with Miss Milbank.

Nottingham The 'Trip to Jerusalem', built in the twelfth century, may well be the oldest inn in England. From its cellars, in October 1330, a secret subterranean passage allowed two dozen friends of the young King Edward III to enter the otherwise virtually impregnable Nottingham Castle. There, they were able to overpower Roger Mortimer, Earl of March, who had been largely responsible for the murder of Edward's father at Berkeley Castle, and to separate him from Isabella, the assassinated King's widow. The ghost of Mortimer, who was hanged at Tyburn, is said now to haunt the subterranean passage, which is close to the dungeon in which the Earl was temporarily imprisoned. The ghost of the queen has reputedly been seen in the Castle, too, crying pitifully and pleading for mercy for her captive lover.

Ollerton   Rufford Abbey, some two miles from Ollerton, is said to be haunted by an exceptionally tall ghost – a monk, probably, with a skull rather than a face inside his cowl. Here, too, visitors have experienced the feeling of a shivering, frightened child cuddling up to them in bed, as though he or she were in need of comfort and protection. Local gossips say that many years ago a real-life child who was being chased through the passages of the Abbey tried to hide in one of the massive bedsteads and was accidentally smothered.

Wellow   This picturesque place has been for many years one of the few in the country to possess a permanent maypole. The ceremonies that traditionally have taken place by the pole in early summer were frowned on by the Puritans, who called them 'laxities'. The origins of the rites were almost certainly pagan, and resemble the fertility rites practised in one form or another in many different parts of the world. The maypole itself is, clearly, a phallic symbol, and one of the dances – 'Amo Amas' – performed by the older Wellow children may be a reminder of Ama, Sumerian mother goddess and creatrix of the seed of mankind, or of the Latin verb meaning 'I love; thou lovest . . .' The celebrations can also be convincingly linked with the Roman goddess Flora.

Further reading
Mayfield, Pat, *Legends of Nottinghamshire*, Dalesman, 1976.

Further information from
The Local Studies Librarian, County Library, Angel Row,
   Nottingham, NG1 6HP.

Oxfordshire

Adderbury A ghostly coach with four horses has been reported in this neighbourhood. It may have been the phantom conveyance of a local landowner who, in the eighteenth century, left instructions that his four favourite oak trees were to be carefully preserved after his death. His wishes were disregarded; the trees were cut down; and the hauntings began.

Ambrosden St Mary's Church here is said to have been built on a site chosen by the Devil. The ecclesiastical authorities intended the church to stand on the field still known as 'Church Leys' and had the foundations dug there, but the materials were moved each night by supernatural means to the church's present location.

Bampton This is one of the principal centres of Morris Dancing in the Midlands – Bampton has had Morris Men performing their ancient rituals in early summer for several centuries. The dancers 'go public' now on the Spring Bank Holiday.

Bloxham The fourteenth-century church spire here is said to have been put up by two brothers who engaged an unknown freelance workman to help them. The stranger worked harder than anyone else; refused to accept any payment; and then disappeared, leaving the brothers convinced that they had had the Devil's assistance.

Dancers recall an ancient ritual

Clifton Hampden   Courtiers House in Clifton Hampden is said
to be haunted by the ghost of an unfortunate young woman who
lived in it at the end of the eighteenth century. Though beautiful,
she was sadly neglected by her heedless husband. Unable to
stand her lonely state eventually she committed suicide in her
bedroom.

Finstock   In nearby Wychwood Forest there is a well known as
'The Lady's Well'. For centuries, on each Palm Sunday, children
from Finstock have drawn water from this well and, having
dissolved some liquorice in it, have enjoyed a drink. Without
knowing exactly what they are doing, they are almost certainly
re-enacting an ancient pagan ritual in a modernised form.

Little Rollright   The Rollright Stones, near here, form a circle
with a diameter of about 100 feet (30m). Near this circle there is
a smaller group, known as 'The Whispering Knights'. Close to
these there is a single megalith known as 'The King Stone'.
According to a local tradition, no one alive can count the stones
three times and reach the same total on each occasion. Another
legend tells that the stones were once an army that had
conquered the whole of England as far north as the village of
Little Rollright. The men were turned to stone by a local witch,
after a particularly tricky bit of sorcery. Sometimes, it is claimed,
the stones come temporarily to life at midnight and perform
strange dances, or ramble off to look for drinking water.

Oddington   The wells here, like others on Otmoor, have long
been celebrated for their healing qualities. The water at
Oddington is supposed to be particularly good for 'Moor Fever',
an ailment that once troubled many of the local cattle.

Oxford   Two Oxford ceremonies, now clearly Christian, may
well have had their origins in some long-forgotten pagan rituals.
At Queen's College, at Christmas, a boar's head is carried into the

Uffington Great White Horse

Hall on a silver dish, and it is followed by the members of the
College choir who sing a traditional carol. On May Day morning
the choristers of Magdalen College climb to the top of the college
tower to sing a Latin carol, after which the bells are rung, and
Morris men dance in the streets.

Uffington   The Uffington White Horse, which gives its name to
the Vale of the White Horse below, is undeniably ancient. It has a
stylised outline which resembles that of a cat or a dragon as much
as that of a horse, but its similarity to representations of horses
on early Celtic coins makes its identity undoubtedly equine. Its
origins are uncertain, but it probably served as the god or totem
of the Celtic tribe which lived near it in the centuries that
immediately preceded the Roman invasion of Britain.

Further reading
Richardson, J., *Oxford and County Ghost Stories*, Hannan, 1977.
Richardson, J., *Thirty-Six Strange Tales from Oxford and Shire*,
    Hannan, 1981.

Further information from
The County Librarian, Central Library, Westgate, Oxford, OX1
    1DJ.

Shropshire

Aston-on-Clun   On what was once the village green, an English
or Native Black Poplar tree has been growing for at least 250
years. (Experts say it may be as much as twice as old as that.)
For more than a century, it has been quite hollow. Since the
restoration of the monarchy in 1660, it has been known as the
'Arbor Tree' and, as such, has been decorated on 29 May in each
year with 'votives' or prayer flags, in accordance with Charles II's
wishes. It is virtually certain that this ceremony, intended to

demonstrate loyalty to the Crown, was based on much earlier rituals intended to honour Breede or Brigid, the Celtic Goddess of Fertility, whose shrine was a tree.

Ellesmere   The largest of the 'meres' or lakes round this town is supposed locally to have had magical origins. In one version of the mere's history, Ellesmere's people are said to have depended for their water supply, long ago, on a well in a field near the town. When the field changed hands, the new owner refused to allow the townspeople free access to the well. They said prayers, or carried out some other mystical process. The well overflowed, the field was flooded, and from that time on there were no difficulties over supplies of free fresh water.

Great Ness   A cave in the side of Nesscliff Hill, near here, is said to have provided shelter for Humphrey Kynaston, a fifteenth-century desperado who, like Robin Hood, robbed the rich so that he could give to the poor. Kynaston's greatest asset was his horse, which was popularly supposed to be an equine incarnation of the Devil. Among the fantastic feats ascribed to this satanic steed was a leap over the Severn at a point at which the river was – and is – nearly 14 yards wide.

Kinlet   A monument in Kinlet Church is dedicated to the memory of Sir George Blount, squire of the district in the sixteenth century. Sir George so disapproved of his daughter's marriage to a servant that he vowed he would haunt her, and her descendants, into the foreseeable future. This drastic treatment seems to have been effective, for in the eighteenth century a group of clergymen had to meet to exorcise Sir George's vindictive spirit, and to imprison it in a bottle.

Middleton-in-Chirbury   A carved capital in the Church of the Holy Trinity, here, shows a witch in a tall hat milking a cow. This is an illustration of an old local tale. Once, when there was a dreadful famine in the district, a fairy cow appeared night and morning in the field known as 'Mitchell's Fold' and waited to be

milked. It did not matter how many people went to milk her – there would always be enough milk for all, as long as everyone who went took only one pailful. At last, a spiteful old witch named Mitchell took a sieve or riddle and milked the cow into that. Of course, the poor creature could not fill it. The witch went on milking her until at last she had milked her dry. The cow vanished after that and was never seen again.

Minsterley   The shade of Wild Edric, heroic leader of Norman times, is said to gallop through the Welsh Marches when war or disaster threatens Britain. The phantom and his ghostly steed were spotted at Minsterley shortly before the outbreak of the Crimean War.

Shrewsbury   The spire of St Alkmond's Church here was badly damaged in a great storm which broke over the building while Mass was being celebrated, on a day just a few years after the Reformation. According to the townspeople, the Devil attacked the church, breaking off one of the stone pinnacles, which is still missing, and leaving the marks of his claws on one of the bells.

Stoke St Milborough   A well near the church is said to have mysterious origins. According to a local story, the Saxon St Milburgh once fell foul of a band of outlaws, and they hunted her over the countryside by day and by night. At last she fell exhausted to the ground. The outlaws' hounds were about to seize her and tear her to pieces when water surged from the earth, putting them off the scent and allowing the saint to escape.

The Wrekin   This great landmark is said locally to have been made by two giants with earth that they dug from the bed of the River Severn. For a time, they lived happily inside the hill. Then, one day, they quarrelled. One of the giants took his spade and aimed a blow at his companion, missed, and made the cleft in the hill known ever since as 'The Needle's Eye'. He was then

The Wrekin, haunt of giants

attacked by the pet raven belonging to the other giant. This pecked out his eyes. The tears he shed formed the pool that is still known as 'The Raven's Bowl'. Being blind and helpless, he was easily knocked unconscious. Shut up by the victorious giant in Ercall Hill, the loser can still sometimes be heard at dead of night, groaning with dismay at his fate.

Further reading

Burne, Charlotte, *Shropshire Folk-Lore: A Sheaf of Gleanings*,
    Trübner and Co., 1883.
Hughes, Jean, *Shropshire Folklore, Ghosts and Witchcraft*, Wilding
    and Son, Shrewsbury, 1975.

Further information from

The Local Studies Department, County Library, Castle Gates,
    Shrewsbury, SY1 2AS.

Somerset

Buckland St Mary   Old folk in this district say that it was once a favourite haunt of fairies, and their last stronghold in the shire.

Cadbury   This 'castle' or Iron Age hill-fort not far from Yeovil has been identified for centuries with the 'many tower'd Camelot' of Arthurian legends. Queen Camel, near the foot of Cadbury Hill, has similarly been nominated as a possible site of the Battle of Camlann, the conflict in which Arthur received his fatal wounds. The hill is one of many places in which the King and his knights are said to lie sleeping. Once every seven years, on Midsummer Eve, a door in the side of the hill is said to open, and the inhabitants of the interior come out and ride down to water their horses at a well near the church at Sutton Montis.

The tor at Glastonbury, Somerset

Combe Sydenham   Within a few decades of his death, Sir Francis
Drake had gained the reputation, in Somerset, of having been a
powerful wizard. One of his most spectacular feats was said to
have been performed when he was returning from one of his
journeys to the Spanish Main. According to a local tradition, he
fired a cannon ball from his ship as it was entering Plymouth
Sound. It landed on the church path at Combe Sydenham, where
his wife, thinking that she had become a widow, was about to
marry another man. The cannon ball is still preserved in the
museum at Taunton.

Dunster   On Christmas Eve, in Somerset, it has been for many
centuries the custom to burn, indoors, bundles of ash branches,
bound with pliant ash twigs. The ceremony has survived at
Dunster into the present decade.

Glastonbury   When the invading Anglo-Saxons reached
Glastonbury in the year 658, they are believed to have found
there a community of monks living in a group of huts round an
old wattle-and-daub church, which had been encased in timber to
protect it. Since then, so many legends have grown about
Glastonbury that it can well claim to be one of the most
mysterious and magical places in Britain.
   The wattle-and-daub church (for a start) has been said to have
belonged to the very earliest age of Christianity, and one account
of its origin says that it was built by the hands of Christ himself,
in the hidden years between his boyhood and the beginning of
his mission. Later, the legend arose that Christ was the nephew
of Joseph of Arimathea, who used to come to Britain to trade in
tin. Then, when the persecution of Christians started in earnest,
Joseph is said to have come to Britain, and safety, with several
followers, and to have brought with him the cup used at the Last
Supper. This became the 'Holy Grail' of Arthurian romance. (See
Capel Seion, **Dyfed**). Joseph's staff, which he is said to have
thrust into the ground at Glastonbury, took root and budded,
and became the 'Glastonbury Thorn' (*Crataegus oxyacantha*) which
is believed to blossom only at Christmas. Trees grown from

cuttings from this still flourish in several parts of Britain, though the original was cut down during the Commonwealth because it was thought to encourage idolatry.

As the Abbey at Glastonbury grew into one of the most powerful and wealthy of all the religious houses in medieval Britain, the place's associations with King Arthur and his entourage became widely publicised. (Possibly because the monks found that these romantic stories helped to bring increasing numbers of pilgrims to Glastonbury.) Of the many strands in the tangled web of Arthurian lore, two may be judged to be most relevant in this context. Melwas, Ruler of the Summer Land (Somerset) is said to have kidnapped Guinevere and to have imprisoned her in his fortress here; Arthur, unable to march with his supporters through the surrounding marshes, could not rescue her, and she had to remain a prisoner until the Abbot of Glastonbury successfully pleaded for her release. Most intriguing, perhaps, of all is the story which tells how Arthur, mortally wounded at the Battle of Camlann, was brought by barge to Glastonbury and, when he died, was buried by the monks in their own cemetery. Here, in the twelfth century, the monks of the time are said to have found a lead cross inscribed with the words '*HIC IACET SEPULTUS INCLYTUS REX ARTURIUS IN INSULA AVALONIA*' or 'Here, in the Isle of Avalon, the famous King Arthur lies buried'. Controversy about the authenticity, or otherwise, of this cross still continues.

Hinton St George   Traces of the ancient rituals connected with the Celtic autumn fire festival 'Samain' seem to have survived here into the present century.

Minehead   Old springtime fertility rites are recalled by the ceremonies held here in early May. Of these, the town's hobby horses are important components. Each hobby horse has an elongated, boat-shaped body, and some people say that this characteristic suggests a possible change in the ritual after the ninth century, when Viking pirates were routed by Minehead sailors. The local men are believed to have gone to sea in a vessel formed and decorated to resemble a sea monster of some kind.

Sedgemoor   The Duke of Monmouth's ill-fated invasion of Somerset in 1685 had such terrible consequences that it is hardly surprising that the area has been believed to be one of the most poignantly haunted in the whole of England. As well as the phantom troops said to have been seen on the battlefield, retreating ignominiously towards the River Cary, the ghosts of hanged men can allegedly be heard choking by the Gallows Tree near Crowcombe, and the tramp of soldiers' feet can be heard in Taunton Castle, where many of the defeated men, and those who gave them shelter, were imprisoned. Judge Jeffreys, who conducted the Bloody Assize, is claimed for a number of sites in Somerset, Devon and Dorset.

Shepton Mallet   The most famous ghost ever seen in the vicinity of Shepton Mallet is said to have been that of the dishonest local innkeeper Giles Cannard. Cannard, alive in the eighteenth century, was finally unmasked in an attempt to rob the townspeople of some common land. A mob of furious men set off for his inn, intending to kill him. Preferring to commit suicide rather than be lynched, Cannard hanged himself. According to the custom of the time, a stake was driven through his heart, and he was buried at the crossroads near the present-day inn that bears his name.

Stogursey   The Bronze Age burial mound known as 'Wick Barrow' has been believed locally to be the home of elves or pixies.

Taunton   See **Sedgemoor**, **Somerset**, above.

Further reading
Palmer, Kingsley, *The Folklore of Somerset*, Batsford, 1976.
Poole, Charles Henry, *The Customs, Superstitions and Legends of the County of Somerset*, Toucan Press, 1970.

Further information from
The Local History Librarian, The Local History Library, The
    Castle, Castle Green, Taunton, TA1 4AD.

South Yorkshire

Hickleton   The ghost of a man on horseback – possibly a
highwayman – has been seen at night near here on several
occasions.

Sheffield   The men and boys of several villages in this area have
enjoyed keeping up the traditional sword-dancing routines
associated, usually, with midwinter. Like the Mummers' Plays of
which, at one time, they may have been part, the dances involve
the pretended death of a central character, and his restoration to
life by a comical and boastful doctor. Many centuries ago, this
would have been intended to persuade the life-giving sun to
return to its 'rightful' place in the heavens.

Wharncliffe Side   According to a ballad printed in 1699 in *Wit
and Mirth: Or, Pills to Purge Melancholy*, this was once the home of
a 'furious knight' named More of More Hall, who could 'kick, cuff
and huff' and could swing a horse by its tail until it died. When
the locals came to him and begged him to save them from the
Dragon of Wantley, which was terrorising the district, More went
to Sheffield and got himself a suit of armour set with spikes,
which made him look like 'a strange outlandish hedgehog'. Thus
protected, and fortified with a pint of brandy and six pots of ale,
More went on the offensive and vanquished the Dragon by
means of a well-aimed kick in the rear.

Further information from
The Local Studies Librarian, Central Library, Surrey Street,
    Sheffield, S1 1XZ.

Staffordshire

Abbots Bromley   Robert Plot, in his *Natural History of
Stafford-shire*, published in 1686, described the extraordinary
dance that still draws fascinated crowds to this small Midlands
town:

> At *Abbots . . . Bromley*, they had also within memory, a sort of
> sport, which they celebrated at *Christmas* (on *New-year*, and
> *Twelft-day*) call'd the *Hobby-horse dance*, from a person that
> carryed the image of a *horse* between his leggs, made of thin
> boards, and in his hand a *bow* and *arrow*, which passing
> through a hole in the bow . . . he made a *snapping* noise as he
> drew it to and fro, keeping time with the *Musick*: with this *Man*
> danced 6 others, carrying on their shoulders as many *Rain deers
> heads*, 3 of them painted *white*, and 3 *red* . . .

Today, the dance or 'running' takes place on a Sunday or
Monday in early September. The dancers start at dawn near the
church and then make a tour of several local farms, where they
are welcomed in the belief that they bring with them good luck
and fertility. They finish during the afternoon with a performance
given in Abbots Bromley's main street.

As well as the fanciful characters known as 'The Bowman',
'The Fool', 'The Hobby Horse' and 'Maid Marian', the troupe
includes three dancers equipped with black reindeer horns, and
three with white (not red, as in Plot's time). At the climax of the
dance, the black and white Deer-men confront each other and,

The Abbots Bromley horn dance

lowering their horns, perform with slow and stately mime the formalised movements of an ancient ritual. It is impossible to tell, now, exactly how old the ceremony is – almost certainly it has survived from pre-Christian times, and equally probably it had, originally, a potent magical significance. It is possible that when the Bowman pretends to hunt the Deer-men, today, he is repeating, more or less, the actions of some Stone Age man who largely relied on such observances to bring success in the chase. Without such success, the primitive hunter and his dependants could hardly hope to survive.

Endon   The custom of 'Well Dressing' is still observed here, during Spring Bank Holiday, as it is in many small towns and villages in Derbyshire. In Endon, as there, the ceremony is probably a reminder of pre-Christian well-worship.

Tamworth   The Castle, which was given to Robert de Marmion by William the Conqueror to reward him for his bravery at the Battle of Hastings, is said to be haunted by two ghosts, both female.

One – known as 'The Black Lady' – is believed to be the restless spirit of one Editha, possibly the sister of the tenth-century King Athelstan. Before she died, Editha founded a convent, and became well known for acts of charity and devotion. When de Marmion and his family took possession of Tamworth Castle, however, he drove the nuns from their convent, which he wanted for his own uses. Called up from her grave by the desperate prayers of her followers, the angry Editha surprised de Marmion in his bedroom and gave him a good beating with her crozier. Her ghost has been seen in this room, and the stairway down which de Marmion staggered, bleeding from his wounds, is still known as the 'Haunted Staircase'.

The second ghost – dressed in white – has been seen, according to reports, on the terrace of the Castle. From there, a distraught lady is supposed to have watched while her lover – Sir Tarquin, a ruthless Saxon knight – was slain by the noble Sir Lancelot du Lake on Lady Meadow, below the Castle. Sir Lancelot is supposed then to have rescued forty knights from inside the stronghold.

Walsall The White Hart Inn at Caldmore Green is only about three hundred years old, but it is believed that timbers from a much older building which previously stood on the site are incorporated in the present fabric.

In 1870, the mummified arm of a child was found, with a Cromwellian sword, in the attic of the inn. This grisly relic – preserved, now, in the Walsall Museum – became known locally as the 'Hand of Glory'. A 'Hand of Glory' was a hand cut from a hanged felon, pickled with certain proven salts and dried in the sun. Such a hand could be used to hold a candle made from the fat of a hanged man, with virgin wax and oil pressed from the seeds of the sesame plant. Light from a candle of this sort was supposed to stupefy any person who saw it, and would enable a burglar to ransack a house without being caught. It was generally believed that the candle's flame could not be blown out by any ordinary person, and that milk was the only liquid that would extinguish it. The macabre origins of the 'Hand of Glory' became less certain in 1965, when a pathologist from the Medical School of Birmingham University asserted that it was, in reality, an anatomical specimen that had once been preserved and partly dissected by some unknown surgeon or student. In spite of this, many strange phenomena have since been experienced at the White Hart.

Further reading
Hackwood, F. W. M., *Staffordshire Customs, Superstitions and Folklore*, E.P. Publishing, 1974.
Raven, Jon, *The Folklore of Staffordshire*, Batsford, 1978.

Further information from
The Principal Area Librarian, City Central Library, Bethesda Street, Hanley, Stoke-on-Trent, ST1 3RS.

Suffolk

Beccles The ghosts of Roos Hall are renowned throughout the county. The Devil is said to have visited this old mansion, too, leaving an identifiable footprint on one of its walls.

Blaxhall A boulder at Stone Farm, Blaxhall, is reputed to be growing steadily, year by year.

Blythburgh The Devil is alleged to have attacked Holy Trinity Church here during the sixteenth century. Bringing with him 'a strange and terrible tempest' he did considerable damage, leaving the marks of his claws on the door as he hurried away.

Bungay At the time of the same 'strange and terrible tempest' that so affected **Blythburgh**, **Suffolk** (see above), the Devil disguised as a black demon dog rushed into Bungay Church. An old pamphlet records that by the time the dog left, two members of the congregation had been strangled, and a third was 'as shrunken as a piece of leather scorched in a hot fire'.

Bury St Edmunds Edmund, King of the East Angles, is believed to have been captured by invading Danes in the ninth century. After refusing to deny his faith, he was beheaded. His soldiers found his body, but could not find his head. After they had searched for it for more than a month, the voice of the martyred king guided them to where it lay, in a dense thicket, resting between the paws of a grey wolf. When the head was replaced on the neck of the torso, the two were mysteriously reunited. The completed body was interred in the Abbey at Bury, but its exact whereabouts are not known.

Dagworth Ralph of Coggeshall, writing in the thirteenth century, recorded that Dagworth Castle was haunted at that time by a child called 'Malekin' who could be seen only by a single servant, but who could be heard by others, and touched. Malekin claimed that she had been born to human parents, but had later been stolen by the fairies while her mother was helping with the harvest, and had been kept by them for the past seven years. The fairy child spoke to the inhabitants of the castle 'according to the idiom of the region', observed Ralph. With the priest, he said, she discussed religious matters in Latin.

Dunwich   Until the fourteenth century, Dunwich was a busy seaport. Then most of the town was submerged, and after further centuries of erosion the place has been even more reduced. Some people now living in the area still listen for the sound of the bells of the drowned town's church, believing that the muffled peals will warn them of approaching storms.

Hoxne   At a bridge near here, Edmund, King of the East Angles, is said to have been betrayed to the Danes during the ninth century. (See **Bury St Edmunds**, **Suffolk**, above.) The King, realising that his hiding-place under the bridge had been discovered and given away by a newly married couple, laid a curse on any couple who might want to pass over the bridge on their way to their wedding. Bridal parties going to Hoxne Church were taking circuitous routes as late as the end of the eighteenth century, according to Edmund Gillingwater, in his *Historical Account of Lowestoft*, published at that time.

Little Cornard   A fifteenth-century chronicle preserved now at Canterbury tells of a mighty battle fought in the year 1449 near this village between two dragons. Both dragons breathed out fire. One was black. The other, which lived normally in Essex, was 'reddish and spotted'. The battle went on for an hour, and the Essex dragon won.

Orford   Ralph of Coggeshall, writing in the thirteenth century, reported that the fishermen of Orford had hauled up in their nets a strange creature that looked like a man with a bald head and a long straggly beard. The merman – if that is what it was – was kept for a time in Orford Castle, where it was fed on fish and appeared to be quite contented with its lot. Then one day, when no one was watching, it slipped back into the sea and was never seen by mortals again.

Stowmarket In late Hanoverian times, this was said to be a place particularly favoured by fairies.

Walberswick A phantom coach drawn by headless horses is said to have been occasionally seen near here, during the past two hundred years. The coachman is, reportedly, negroid. He is thought to be (in shade form) Thomas Gill, a black military drummer who, during the eighteenth century, murdered a local white girl and was caught and hanged from a tree in Toby's Walk.

Woolpit This place gets its name from the pits dug here in the early Middle Ages to trap the local wolves. It is of great interest to students of magic, because here, in the twelfth century (according to Ralph of Coggeshall and other learned writers), two fairy children were found, having emerged from the interior of the earth. Both were clad from head to foot in green, and had green skin. They were adopted by the kindly villagers, who tried to feed them. At first, they would eat only beans. Then the male 'green child' slowly dwindled and died. The female, probably of a stronger constitution, started to eat normal human food of all kinds, thrived, became noticeably less green, married a man from Kings Lynn, and lived happily with him for many years.

Further reading
Gurdon, Lady E. C., *County Folk-lore*, *Suffolk*, The Folk-Lore Society and D. Nutt, London, 1893.

Further information from
The County Archivist, St Andrew House, County Hall, Ipswich, IP4 2JS.

Surrey

Albury Silent Pool, a little to the east of Guildford, is a favourite beauty spot. The pool was once said to be bottomless, and to be one of the entrances to the Underworld. Springs near it have for many centuries been regarded as sacred.

Buckland Red stains on a rock near Buckland used to be said to be traces of blood. The blood was supposedly that of the victims of a horrifying water monster known as the 'Buckland Shag'. The Shag vanished for ever when a courageous Vicar of Buckland dared to perform a service of exorcism by the rock.

Coldharbour Maggs Well, in a wood close to the town, has been renowned for centuries for its healing qualities. It has been used as a wishing well, too; those who have wanted to use it in this way have had to drop coins into its waters before stating their requirements.

Cranleigh The ghost of St Thomas More is said to have been frequently seen at Baynards Park, some two miles from the town. The saint's head was certainly brought here by his daughter, Margaret Roper, some time after his execution. The head was on its way to Canterbury.

Epsom Pitt Place (now demolished) was in 1779 the home of the dissolute Thomas, Baron Lyttelton, who was alleged to have two beautiful girls staying in his home brazenly sharing his favours. In a peculiarly vivid dream, one night, he saw an apparition which warned him that he had only three days to live. The prophecy was fulfilled almost to the moment when, three days later, Lord Lyttelton suffered an apoplectic fit at his home and expired. The doomed man is said to have made a mysterious appearance at exactly that time at the home of a friend of his – Miles Peter Andrews, Esquire – at Dartford in Kent, saying, clearly, 'It's all over with me, Andrews'. Doctor Samuel Johnson was much impressed by this and said that it was the most extraordinary instance of supernatural phenomena he had ever come across.

Farnham   Several ghosts have been associated with Farnham Castle. Among them are the shade of a priest or monk said to have been seen in the Long Gallery, overlooking the Great Hall; an unidentified and shadowy female form that has been glimpsed in the Castle gateway; and the ghost of a small child said to have been made to dance herself to death in the Hall. The Parish Church, too, is renowned for its ghostly choir, said to chant services in Latin in the dark, empty church. And the hooves of phantom horses are said several times to have been heard approaching the Hop Bag Inn (formerly the 'Adam and Eve') in Downing Street. According to a local tradition, the sound reminds those who hear it of a poor girl who waited at the inn for her lover, due to arrive as a passenger on a coach from London. When the coach reached Farnham, the driver had to break the news to the girl that her lover had been killed on the journey by a highwayman.

Frensham   A large iron cauldron in St Mary's Church is said by some to have belonged, once, to a witch of benevolent temper called Mother Ludlam who used to live in a spacious cave in the grounds of Moor Park. The good lady used to lend to her poor neighbours anything they wanted, the story goes on, but when someone who had borrowed the cauldron failed to return it within the allotted time Mother Ludlam refused to take it back and disappeared for ever from human sight. This unlikely story seems to have taken the place of an even older tale in which the kind lenders were the local fairies. They, too, took umbrage when their cauldron failed to come back to them on time.

Godalming   The grounds of Westbrook Place are said to be haunted by the ghost of the Young Pretender, who is believed to have visited the mansion just before the 1745 Rebellion. The wraith walks only in the twilight – presumably for security reasons – and hides himself as far as possible in a voluminous cloak.

Guildford The ghost of Christopher Slaughterford is said to have been seen and heard frequently near the sandpits by the footpath that leads from Guildford to Polesden. Slaughterford was hanged on 9 July 1709 for the murder of Jane Young, his sweetheart, after vehemently protesting his innocence. An eighteenth-century broadsheet tells how Slaughterford's ghost appears 'with a Rope around his neck, a flaming torch in one hand and a club in the other' and cries 'Vengeance, Vengeance, Vengeance'.

In the town's centre there are at least two buildings that are reputedly haunted. The shop at 122 High Street, which dates from 1670, has above it rooms in which are heard slow halting footsteps that suggest that someone is moving with great difficulty across the floor. In a room at the famous Angel Hotel, a figure in military uniform has appeared in a mirror and has remained visible long enough for the room's occupant to make a sketch of the unexpected visitor.

Leatherhead A mysterious figure clothed in a long gown of rough material like hessian has more than once appeared in the old Parish Church. It was seen by a Rev. Coleridge, a descendant of the poet, who was careful at first not to report his experience in public lest the members of his congregation should be scared of using the church for private meditation and prayers.

Pyrford A large stone near the entrance to Pyrford Court was said to turn in its setting when the cock crowed at dawn.

Shepperton The ghost of a headless monk has been several times sighted in and around Shepperton. The restless figure may be associated with one of the monks from Chertsey Abbey who left the community to live with a woman on a riverside farm. He was hunted down by more faithful members of his Order, it is believed, and beheaded.

Walton-on-Thames   The Manor House was built – at least in part – in the fifteenth century. It has been the home of two famous judges: John Bradshaw, President of the Council which sent Charles I to the block; and Lord Chief Justice Jeffreys, hated protagonist of the Bloody Assize. One of these – it is uncertain which – is said to have revisited his old home from time to time, in ghostly guise.

Weybridge   Not much of the old motor racing circuit at Brooklands, near Weybridge, has survived, but the area is said still to be disturbed, on certain nights, by sounds reminiscent of the track in its heyday.

Further reading
Alexander, M., *Tales of Old Surrey*, Countryside Books, 1985.
Green, A. M., *Mysteries of Surrey*, Napier Publications,
    Walton-on-Thames, 1972.

Further information from
The Local Studies Library, Branch Library, North Street,
    Guildford, Surrey, GU1 4AL.

Tyne and Wear

Hylton Castle   Here, the fifteenth-century tower house has been considerably enlarged in more recent times. It used to be haunted by a spirit known as the 'Cauld Lad of Hilton'. According to several local historians, the servants who used to sleep in the Castle's Great Hall would hear the Cauld Lad working each night in the kitchen. As was usual with domesticated brownies of the kind, the Cauld Lad tended to tidy the things that were untidy, and to leave all that had previously been tidy in a mess. At last the human servants decided to get rid of their supernatural associate and, following the traditional recipe for banishing brownies, they left a green cloak and hood for him by the kitchen fire. From a place of concealment, they saw the Cauld Lad come in, look at the clothes with much delight, and put them on. At cock-crow, he disappeared for ever, shouting:

> *Here's a cloak and here's a hood,*
> *The Cauld Lad of Hilton will do no more good.*

Further reading
History of the Cauld Lad of Hilton (Chiefly from Surtees' *History of Durham*), T. Arthur, York; facsimile published by Frank Graham, 6 Queen's Terrace, Newcastle upon Tyne, NE2 2PL.

Further information from
The County Archivist, Archives Department, Blandford House, West Blandford Street, Newcastle upon Tyne, NE1 4JA.

Warwickshire

Edge Hill   The Battle of Edge Hill, fought in October 1642 between the armies of Charles I and the Parliamentarians, is said to have been refought by phantom warriors on several occasions during the following months. In *A Great Wonder in Heaven*, published early in 1643, a pamphleteer recorded 'the sound of drummes afar off, and the noyse of souldiers, as it were, giving out their last groanes'. The writer declared that these manifestations showed God's wrath against the land for the civil wars.

Guy's Cliffe   This sandstone cliff a little to the north of Warwick contains a cave in which the legendary hero Guy of Warwick is said to have spent his last days. Guy is best known for the daring deeds he carried out in order to prove his love for the fair Felice, daughter of the Earl of Warwick of the time. In one famous adventure he fought and slew the gigantic Wild Dun Cow which had been intimidating the people of Dunsmore Heath, near

Stretton-on-Dunsmore. The cow, a supernatural creature, had previously been benevolent, and, in times of famine, had blessed the locals with an apparently endless supply of milk. Its nature changed, however, when a witch managed by magic to milk it dry. Then, it started man-eating.

Long Lawford   The Hall Farm here stands on the site of Lawford Hall, demolished more than a century ago. During the sixteenth century, the Hall was the home of members of the Boughton Family, one of whom had lost an arm. His ghost was said to haunt the Hall. After the building was pulled down, he was believed to ride round the district in a phantom coach.

Warwick   The Castle is said to be haunted by the ghost of Sir Fulke Greville. On a slightly less aristocratic level, a seventeenth-century landlord of the Anchor Inn is said to have been carried off, for his dishonesty, by the Devil. No trace of the landlord was left but 'a terrible stinke'.

Wroxall Abbey   The ruined priory here is said to have been founded by a Hugh de Hatton, who was taken prisoner while he was on a Crusade in the Holy Land. When he had spent seven weary years in captivity and had little hope of ever regaining his freedom, Hugh prayed to St Leonard, to whom his local church in England was dedicated. Promptly, St Leonard appeared and told Hugh to return to England, There, by his church at Wroxall, Hugh was to found a religious house for females of the Benedictine Order. Without understanding how this was to be made possible, Hugh was miraculously transported, still in his chains, to the woods near Wroxall. Overgrown with hair, he was not immediately recognised, but (according to Sir William Dugdale, in his *The Antiquities of Warwickshire*, published in 1656)

> . . . his Lady and Children, having advertisement, came forthwith to him, but believed not that he was her husband, till he shewed her a piece of a Ring, that had been broken betwixt them . . .

Further reading
Atkins, Meg Elizabeth, *Haunted Warwickshire*, Hale, 1981.
Bloom, J. Harvey, *Folklore, Old Customs and Superstitions in Shakespeareland*, reprinted by E.P. Publishing, 1976.
Palmer, Roy, *The Folklore of Warwickshire*, Batsford, 1976.

Further information from
The Librarian, Warwick Library, Barrack Street, Warwick, CV34 4TH.

West Midlands

Bilston The medieval ceremony known as 'Waking' or 'The Wakes' required the people of a village or town to take candles into their churchyard on the eve of the Feast Day of the church's patron saint. There, they would keep a vigil for the dead. Probably this old ceremony was itself a distorted survival of an even older ritual. The midsummer Bilston Carnival, enjoyed in the later decades of the twentieth century, has evolved from the ceremony previously repeated here on the eve of each St Leonard's Day, in early November.

Coventry The well-known story of Lady Godiva, who rode naked through Coventry's marketplace as some kind of penance for the misdeeds of her husband, may recall an ancient fertility rite held locally, in which the ceremony would have been presided over by a naked goddess, or by a woman representing one.

West Sussex

Amberley People living in the vicarage here used to see the ghosts of an old man and of a little girl, apparently aged about seven. Earlier in this century, two skeletons – one fully-grown, one small – were found under a rough board in a cupboard in the dining-room. After the bones were given Christian burial, the hauntings ceased.

Arundel In the castle here there is a long sword called 'Morglay'. It is believed to have been used by the giant Bevis, one time Warden of the Castle. Bevis was so tall that he could walk over the seabed from the mainland to the Isle of Wight without wetting his head.

Bosham The tenor bell of the church at Bosham is said to have been stolen by Danish pirates during the tenth century. As they sailed away with it, members of the monastic community on shore started to ring the bells that the Danes had left. The tenor bell on the boat joined in the peal in the usual way, causing so much disruption by its movements that the boat sank, and the thieving pirates were drowned. Many Bosham people think that the bell still lies submerged, not far from the present church, and that when the bells are rung on shore, the tenor bell chimes in, below.

Bramber Ghostly children seen begging in the streets here are believed to be the young de Breones, starved to death at Windsor while hostages of King John.

Cuckfield A lime tree in Cuckfield Park was believed to shed a branch when any member of the family living in the big house was about to die.

Kingley Vale A grove of ancient yew trees in Kingley Vale, near Chichester, is said by some experts to mark the site of a ninth-century battle. In this fight the local citizens defeated a large force of Viking invaders, slew many hundreds of them, and put the survivors to flight. Other experts say that the trees originally planted here would have been old long before the Vikings arrived, and they think that this, in pre-Christian times, would have been a sacred grove of some kind. Some people who live in the neighbourhood allege that at night the trees change their shapes and move surreptitiously round the Vale.

Lyminster A pool near the north-west corner of the churchyard has been thought, for centuries, to be bottomless. (Modern researchers have discovered that the water in it is actually about thirty feet deep.) In the olden days, the pool was thought to be the home of a legendary monster called a 'Knucker', whose favourite food was attractive maidens. The beast ate all the pretty girls around, until one only was left, and she was the daughter of the King of Sussex. The King, anxious not to lose the girl, offered to give her in marriage, with half his kingdom, to anyone who could manage to kill the Knucker. The challenge was accepted by a courageous knight, who fought and slew the beast. The young couple then got married and set up house in the district. An early Norman memorial tablet in Lyminster Church is said locally to have covered the knight's grave in the churchyard. It was moved to the inside of the building to protect it from further wear and tear.

Poling The solemn chanting of phantom Knights Hospitallers has reputedly been heard at Poling Priory, parts of which date from the twelfth century.

Steyning A memorial stone in Steyning Church is said to have been used originally to cover the grave, somewhere in the churchyard, of the eighth-century Saint Cuthman. When he was young, Cuthman is believed to have travelled through Sussex, preaching the gospel. His old mother was sick and he was unwilling to leave her, so he took her with him, drawing her along in a cart. When the pair reached Penfolds Field at Steyning, the cart fell to bits and the old woman was thrown to the ground. People making hay nearby laughed at this. Cuthman, annoyed at their lack of feeling, put a curse on the field. The curse was effective – rain fell in torrents, and spoiled the hay of those who had mocked. Even now, the mowing of Penfolds Field is said invariably to bring bad weather.

Further reading
Candlin, L., *Tales of Old Sussex*, Countryside Books, 1985.
Simpson, J., *The Folklore of Sussex*, Batsford, 1973.

Further information from
The Librarian-in-Charge, Western Divisional Library, 1A East
   Row, Chichester, West Sussex.

West Yorkshire

Barwick-in-Elmet   England's tallest maypole has been standing, over a period of many years, at the centre of Barwick-in-Elmet. Each Whit Tuesday there is a procession, followed by maypole dancing and a crowning ceremony for the May Queen. There is little doubt that these rites had their origins in ancient fertility ceremonies.

Bradford   The Theatre Royal is supposed to be haunted by the ghost of the great actor Sir Henry Irving, who collapsed and died here on 13 October 1905.

Dewsbury   Sir Thomas de Soothill, who lived in Dewsbury in the thirteenth century, is believed to have murdered a young servant and to have thrown his body into a dammed stream. As a penance for his crime, Sir Thomas was made to present a tenor bell to the parish church of All Saints.
   In recent centuries, Dewsbury has held an important place in bell-ringing circles, for on each Christmas Eve, except in wartime, 'The Devil's Knell' has been tolled. The ringers begin at a few

minutes after 11 o'clock on Christmas Eve and, tolling at thirty-five strokes to the minute, they toll the tenor bell once for every year since the birth of Christ. By careful timekeeping, they manage to complete the process so that the last stroke comes exactly as the old parish church clock starts to chime midnight. This is said to ensure that the Devil will be kept away from the parish for the next twelve months.

Elland   The Fleece Inn, and Dog Lane not far away, are both said to be haunted by the ghost of a tough-skinned old vagrant who was brutally murdered in one of the inn's upstairs rooms.

Gawthorpe   The people of Gawthorpe annually revive ancient May Day rituals.

Leeds   This was the home of Mary Bateman, the famous witch who in the early nineteenth century prophesied threateningly though incorrectly the imminent return of Christ. In 1809 she was accused of murdering 'by the administration of poison' a dupe named Rebecca Perigo, of Bramley, who was 'supposed to labour under an evil wish'. Bateman is said to have held Mrs Perigo and her husband completely in her toils, 'now exciting their hopes, then rousing their fears, but all the time draining their purse'. She was found guilty, and hanged at York. When the witch's body was returned to Leeds for exhibition in a gibbet, fortune hunters are said to have torn all the flesh off her bones, since they believed that pieces of witch meat would bring them good luck. Her skeleton is preserved in the city's Medical School.

The gatehouse of ruined Kirkstall Abbey, near Leeds, is believed to be haunted by the ghost of an elderly abbot. Temple Newsham House, also near the city, is said to be haunted by several ghosts. The wraith with a shawl over her shoulders seen by the late Lord Halifax is the best authenticated of them.

Wakefield   When Mary Bolles of Heath Hall, near Wakefield, was about to die in 1661, she requested in her will that the room in which she had breathed her last should be kept permanently closed. For half a century, her wishes were respected. Then the room was reopened. At once, the ghost of Mary Bolles started to haunt the Hall most alarmingly. Since World War Two, the building has been demolished, but the door of the fatal bedroom was carefully preserved. It can be seen now in the Wakefield Museum.

Further information from
The Local History Librarian, Central Library, Municipal
    Buildings, Leeds, LS1 3AB.

Wiltshire

Avebury   This village is almost surrounded by one of the largest and most important prehistoric monuments in Europe. Built nearly four thousand years ago, the monument consists of a circle formed by nearly a hundred upright megaliths, some of which weigh more than fifty tons. The circle is enclosed by a bank and ditch, the whole making a complex nearly five hundred yards across. Further standing sarsens, arranged in pairs, define the Avenue which leads from Avebury to the Sanctuary, a lesser temple on nearby Overton Down.

The purpose of the Bronze Age remains at Avebury is still undecided. Probably the temple was used for fertility rites of some kind, or for generally appeasing the gods. There is no direct evidence that humans or animals were sacrificed here, but they may have been. Whatever its function in the remote past, there is little doubt that it attracted devout pilgrims from all parts of Britain.

Upright stones at Avebury, in Wiltshire

Broad Hinton   A monument in the church here shows Sir
Thomas Wroughton and his wife kneeling in prayer. With them
are smaller figures representing Sir Thomas's four children.
Unusually, this sixteenth-century landowner and his offspring
have no hands. They lost them, according to a local tradition,
after Sir Thomas returned home one day to find that his supper
was not ready. Instead of cooking, his wife had been reading her
Bible. In a fury, Sir Thomas took the Good Book from her and
threw it on the fire. For this sacrilegious deed, the hasty man was
duly punished – his hands and those of his children withered
away. Lady Wroughton, who managed to pull her Bible from the
flames before it was consumed, had her hands badly burned in
the process.

Cley Hill   The ancient fortifications on this hill near Warminster
are believed locally to have been brought into existence by the
Devil who dropped here a load of earth he had been intending to
unload on Devizes.

Hackpen Hill   This has been believed locally to be the home of
fairies.

Langley Burrell   Steinbrook Hill, near here, is said to be haunted
by the ghost of a fifteenth-century Lord of the Manor who, for
religious reasons, was slowly roasted to death on its summit.

Littlecote   Towards the end of the sixteenth century, a masked
man is said to have thrown a newly-born baby on to a fire in
Littlecote House. The midwife, though blindfolded when taken
to and from the house, was able to identify the place where the
inhuman act had been perpetrated and the Lord of the Manor –
a man called 'Wild' Darrell – was arrested. He was tried, but in
spite of the testimony offered by the midwife, he was acquitted.
Fourteen years later, in 1589, while he was riding in Littlecote
Park, Darrell was thrown from his horse and killed. It was widely
believed that the horse had been startled by the sudden
appearance of a burning babe. This piteous phantom is thought

still to haunt the spot – known, to this day, as 'Darrell's Stile'. The mother of the child is said to haunt a corridor in Littlecote House. She may have been 'Wild' Darrell's sister.

Odstock   The gipsy called 'Joshua Scamp' was buried here. Scamp was hanged – many said wrongfully – in Salisbury in 1801, having been suspected of horse-stealing. When gipsies were excluded from the surroundings of Odstock Church, their 'Queen' cursed the Rector and the other church officials. All of them died prematurely or suffered some severe misfortune.

Potterne   A witch who lived here was said to be able to turn herself into a greyhound.

Purton   Watkins' Corner between Purton and Purton Stoke got its name because a man named Watkins was hanged here for murder. Later, his father confessed that he, not his son, had committed the deed. The ghost of the younger Watkins is said to revisit the scene of his unjust end.

Salisbury   Large white birds are said to appear in the neighbourhood when a Bishop of Salisbury is about to die.

Tall effigies called 'The Giant' and 'Hobnob' used to be featured in pagan festivals. They are now in the Salisbury Museum.

Silbury   The great landmark known as 'Silbury Hill' is thought to be the largest man-made mound in Europe – it is 130 feet high and covers 5 acres (approximately 2 hectares). There is little doubt that it was raised for religious or magical purposes, and it was almost certainly closely associated with nearby **Avebury, Wiltshire** (q.v., above). A monarch in golden armour called 'King Sil' or 'King Seal' is reputed to be sitting upright on his horse somewhere in the inside of the hill, but in spite of thorough and protracted archaeological excavations he has not yet been found. His ghost is said to ride round the base of the hill on moonlit nights.

Annually, on Palm Sunday, people used to climb to the top of

Silbury Hill to enjoy some alfresco fun, and to eat fig cakes and
drink sugar and water. This custom may have been intended as
light relief after the hardships of Lent, or it may have had more
distant, more magical, origins.

Stonehenge   According to Geoffrey of Monmouth in his *Histories
of the Kings of Britain*, compiled in the twelfth century, the great
boulders that compose Stonehenge were found on a mountain in
Ireland called 'Killaurus', having been carried there by giants
'from the furthest ends of Africa'. Merlin the magician knew all
about them, Geoffrey claimed, and said of them:

> . . . In these stones is a mystery . . . and a healing virtue
> against many ailments . . . Not a stone is there that lacketh in
> virtue of witchcraft . . .

It is known today that the stones were not brought from
Ireland by Merlin with 'his own engines', or, as many Wiltshire
people have believed, by the Devil, who – they like to think –
carried them across the sea one by one in a single night. Scientists
have shown that the big sarsen stones came, almost certainly,
from the Marlborough Downs, not far away, while the smaller
'blue' stones were brought from the Prescelly Mountains in South
Wales, rafts and rollers being used for the movement of these
considerable loads across water and land respectively.

The building of Stonehenge seems to have taken place in a
number of distinct phases. In the first, a bank and ditch were
made round a circle of small pits, called now the 'Aubrey Holes'
after the man who first made the world aware of them. At more
or less the same time, the 'Heel Stone' which lies outside the
circular embankment was incorporated into the complex. In the
second phase of building, which began nearly four thousand
years ago, the stone circles at the centre of the site were
constructed. At more or less the same time, the processional
route known as 'The Avenue', which leads from the River Avon

Part of Stonehenge

to the great shrine, was laid out. In the third and final phase, local sarsen stones were used for constructing the inner and outer sets of 'trilithons', which resemble great stone goalposts.

The purpose of Stonehenge remains obscure. Some say that it was primarily a temple, where priests used to practise ritual human sacrifice. Others say that it was regarded by the ancients as the door to the Underworld. Recent authorities have suggested that the stones may have been used to calculate the movements of the sun, the moon and other heavenly bodies. Whichever view is right, Stonehenge will continue to attract awed admirers into the foreseeable future.

Wansdyke   This great earthwork used to run right across Wiltshire. Its name, originally, may have been 'Wodnes Dic', or Woden's Ditch. It was probably constructed by the Saxons before they were converted to Christianity, so the name was almost certainly chosen to commemorate their pagan god.

Wilcot   The village is said to be haunted by the ghost of a Dame Anne Wroughton, who was wrongly suspected by her husband of infidelity and was turned out into the snow to die.

Wilcot Manor is reputedly revisited by a monk who was one of the last to live there at the time of the Dissolution of the Monasteries. He hanged himself, rather than leave his old home.

Winterslow   In the early nineteenth century, this was the home of the notorious witch Lydia Shears. She is said to have teased a local farmer by turning herself into a hare, and by drawing his greyhounds towards her own garden where, after entering her own premises, she would disappear. At last the exasperated farmer sought the advice of the Rector of Tytherley. That good man advised the farmer to make a bullet from a silver sixpence. The farmer did so, and with it shot dead the tantalising hare. The witch was then found dead in her cottage with a silver bullet in her heart.

Further reading

Chadwick, John C., *Folklore and Witchcraft in Dorset and Wiltshire*,
    N.J. Clarke Publications, Lyme Regis, 1984.
Whitlock, Ralph, *The Folklore of Wiltshire*, Batsford, 1976.

Further information from

The Director, Wiltshire County Council Library and Museum
    Service, Bythesea Road, Trowbridge, BA14 8BS.

Wales

Clwyd

Denbigh The Castle, now in ruins, was at one time haunted by a fierce dragon, or so it is locally believed. The beast was killed by a man who had eight fingers and two thumbs on each hand.

Gwytherin St Winifred, heroine of Holywell, Clwyd (q.v.), finished her days as Abbess of Gwytherin and was buried in the local churchyard. Her remains were moved to Shrewsbury Abbey in 1138.

Holywell In the seventh century Winifred, or 'Gwenfrewi', was the daughter of a local prince named Tewyth. Her uncle was St Beuno. One day Caradoc, a chieftain from Hawarden, tried to seduce Winifred. She ran from him towards the church built by her uncle. Caradoc ran after her and cut off her head. Where her head stopped rolling, water sprang from the ground – or so it was said. St Beuno came out from the church, took up her head, and placed it back on her body. He then prayed and restored her to life. A white scar thereafter encircled her neck, providing clear proof of her martyrdom. Caradoc – cursed, with his descendants, by St Beuno – sank into the ground and was never seen again. Winifred became a nun, and after her uncle's departure for the Monastery of Clynnog Fawr she joined a community at Gwytherin and became its Abbess. Pilgrims have visited St Winifred's Holy Well, in search of miraculous cures, during many generations, and still do, though it is said that the well's waters come now from the town's supply.

Llandulas The Devil is said to have lived in a cave on Pen y Cefn Mount. From there, he terrorised the people of Llandulas, being particularly vexing to pregnant women. During a service of exorcism held outside the cave, the Devil fell into a deep, muddy pool – which is said to account for his subsequent blackness.

Llandysilio-yn-Iol   The Pillar of Eliseg near the ruins of Valle Crucis Abbey formerly carried an inscribed message that forecast the blessing of the Lord upon all the region of Powys (q.v.) until the day of doom.

Llanelian-yn-Rhos   St Elian's Well here was until early this century feared throughout Wales – it was used for bringing disasters of all kinds to anyone that malignant persons might wish to harm. To operate the curse, the name of the victim had to be written on paper and a crooked pin had to be pushed through it. The keeper of the well would then write the victim's initials on a pebble, which was dropped into the water. The victim was supposed to remain under the curse for as long as the pebble remained in the water. The well is now carefully hidden so that its evil influences can no longer be used as a source of profit by any custodian.

Llanferres   Twelve hundred or more years ago, all the dogs for miles around are said to have collected by a ford in the River Alun, and to have barked furiously at some one or something. A prince had sufficient courage to investigate, and found, washing herself in the river, the daughter of the King of the Underworld. The couple made love and, nine months later, the princess produced a son and a daughter – the first members of her family to be sired by any Christian.

Not far from this ford – known now as 'Rhyd y Gyfarthfa' or 'The Ford of the Barking' – there is, by the side of the old turnpike road, a roughly dressed boulder that measures about 3 feet by 2 feet. To protect it, a stone arch has been built. The name given to the boulder – 'Carreg Carn March Arthur' or 'The Stone of Arthur's Horse's Hoof' – suggests that here Arthur's horse descended from a flying leap taken from the summit of Moel Fammau, about three miles away. If one looks carefully, a large horseshoe-shaped impression can be seen in the surface of the boulder.

St Winifred's well at Holywell, North Wales

Llangar   The site of this old church – remote from any village, and without a proper road to it – is said to have been dictated to its builders by the mysterious appearance of a great white hart.

Llangollen   The Iron Age hill fort near here known as 'Dinas Bran' has, within it, the remains of a medieval castle. Some experts have suggested that this may be one of the most exciting and mysterious places mentioned in Arthurian legend: the Castle of the Grail, stronghold of the lame Fisher King.

Llan Sain Sior   Water from the well in the village of St George near Denbigh has been used since time immemorial and until quite recently for blessing horses, and for curing them of their ailments.

Nannerch   The hill called 'Moel Arthur' between this village and the Vale of Clwyd is said to have treasure buried near its summit. Supernatural lights may guide bold seekers to the place of concealment, but anyone who tries to dig for the wealth is said to be sure to be driven away by thunder, lightning and tempest.

Ruthin   The Maen Huail, or 'Stone of Huail', to be seen in the market place of this old town, is said to have been used as an execution block by King Arthur's supporters when the king wanted his rival Huail dispatched.

Trelawnyd   The large cairn – 'Gop Carn' – on the hill Bryn-y-Saethau ('Hill of the Arrows') has been said to mark the grave of Boudicca, Queen of the Iceni. Ghostly Roman soldiers have been seen here, however, even as late as this century, which would seem to indicate that this may be, instead, the burial place of a Roman general or some other important Roman figure.

Further reading
Jones, T. G., *Welsh Folklore and Folk-Custom*, Methuen, 1930.
Radford, K., *Tales of North Wales*, Skilton and Shaw, 1982.

Further information from
The Local History Librarian for Clwyd, County Civic Centre,
   Mold, CH7 6NW.

Dyfed

Borth   When tides are very low here, the remnants of an ancient forest, now normally submerged, can be seen. Somewhere to the west of Borth is the lost land of Cantre'r Gwaelod, inundated many hundreds of years ago, or so local folk believe.

Bosherton   The lily-ponds here are said to have provided King Arthur with the magic sword Excalibur. The cave known as 'The Devil's Blowhole', on the coast, gets its name from the jets of spray sent skywards when sea and weather conditions are suitable.

Brynberian   A Neolithic gallery grave near here is known as 'Bedd-yr-Afanc' or 'Grave of the Monster'. According to a local tradition the monster was dragged from the water near Brynberian bridge, but nobody now knows how big it was, or its true identity.

Capel Seion   The big house Nanteos was for a long time the home of part of a wooden cup, said by some to have been the Holy Grail used by Christ at the Last Supper. The precious relic is supposed to have been cherished, until the Reformation, by the monks of Strata Florida Abbey.

Carmarthen   This is alleged to have been the birthplace of Merlin the wizard. Near the top of Bryn Myrrdin ('Merlin's Hill'), a little to the east of Carmarthen, there is a chair-like rock on which Merlin is said to have sat while he pronounced his famous

prophecies. Somewhere in the hill there is thought to be a secret cave in which the wizard is kept, still alive, in an enchanted state.

Carreg Cennen   At the end of a cave by the castle, there is a well that was once believed to have magical properties. To make a wish come true, a pin had to be thrown into the water.

Cwrt Y Cadno   Here, near Pumpsaint, lived the famous wizard Doctor Harries. One of his books containing magical instructions was said to be so dangerous that the Doctor had to keep it chained up and padlocked. He would consult it only once a year, and then only in the presence of a fellow wizard from Pencader. The two men would take the book into the woods and would draw a circle round themselves before they dared open it. Inevitably, a violent storm would break and would soak the learned pair.

Devil's Bridge   Three bridges cross the picturesque ravine of the River Mynach. The lowest of the three is said to have been built by the Devil when an old woman's cow was on the wrong side of the gorge. In return for giving the old woman a chance to retrieve her cow, the Devil told her that he wanted the first living creature to use the bridge. She agreed to the bargain, but when the bridge was completed she threw a piece of bread across. Her dog ran after it, and the Devil was cheated of the human soul for which he craved.

Gorslas   On the mountain called 'Mynydd Mawr', near here, is Llyn Llech Owain, or 'The Lake of Owain's Stone Slab'. The pool was once only a magic well. This well would never run dry as long as a stone slab was replaced over it, whenever water had been drawn. One day the keeper of the well – some say it was one of King Arthur's knights – forgot to replace the slab. The well overflowed, and the countryside around was flooded. As the floods spread, the alarmed keeper jumped on his horse and

The cataracts at Devil's Bridge, in Mid-Wales

galloped round them. The hooves of the horse checked the water's flow and established the shape of the present lake.

Hawton   In the estuary of the Towy, near Ferryside, there is said to be a drowned village. At times, according to local reports, the old church bell can be heard tolling.

Kidwelly   The countryside round Kidwelly Castle is said to have been haunted for several centuries by a headless ghost – the shade, presumably, of Gwenllian, wife of Prince Gruffydd ap Rhys ap Tewdwr, who was beheaded in 1136 as she led an attack on this Norman stronghold. The hauntings continued until Gwenllian's skull was found and reunited with the rest of her skeleton.

Llanarth   According to a tale enjoyed locally, the Devil once tried to steal the bell from Llanarth Church. The Vicar, woken by the noise, managed with a bell, book and candle to drive the Devil to the top of the tower, from where the Evil One was forced to jump. In the graveyard there is a stone which still bears the marks said to have been made by the fugitive as he landed.

Llanarthney   A poltergeist caused much trouble, early in this century, at the Emlyn Arms.

Llandeilo   St Teilo's Well, near Maenclochog, used to be visited by many pilgrims, being especially favoured by those suffering from whooping cough or consumption. For the cure to work, the water from the well had to be drunk from the skull of St Teilo, who died in the sixth century. This would be handed to each patient by the heir of the nearby farm. The skull disappeared, mysteriously, in 1927.

Llanddewi Brefi   The church stands on a mound said to have been miraculously raised in the year 519 when St David arrived to address an assembly of bishops and other clerics on the spot. As the saint, suitably elevated, started to speak a white dove flew down and perched on his shoulder.

When two oxen were dragging stones up a steep slope to the site for the building of the church, one of them died. The other is said to have bellowed three times. The hill then split in two, giving an easier path for the survivor to follow.

Llanfihangel Abercywyn Graves in the churchyard are said to be those of pilgrims who died of poverty and starvation. When the graves were neglected, the neighbourhood became notorious for its poisonous snakes. Eventually, a clergyman found the graves and tended them. The snakes returned to the river.

Llangathen Aberglasney, the nearby estate, has the reputation of being cursed. The ghosts of six young girls who died from being accidentally suffocated are said to walk in the grounds.

Myddfai The mountain lake called 'Llyn y Fan Fach' some five miles south of Myddfai has a magical history. During the twelfth century a young man was tending his flocks by the lake when he saw a most beautiful fairy. He wanted to marry her, and he was allowed to do so, but there was a condition attached – if he were to strike her three times, or touch her with iron, she would go back into the waters of the lake, taking with her the beasts she had brought as her dowry.

For some years the pair lived together happily at Esgair Llaethdy, near Myddfai, and had three sons. Then, the young husband is said to have struck his wife twice – once, for crying at a wedding; the second time, for laughing at a funeral. When, after that, he accidentally touched her with the metal bit of a horse's bridle, she called her animals and took them with her into the lake.

As the fairy's three sons grew up, they went repeatedly to Llyn y Fan Fach, hoping to see their mother. Eventually she returned and told the eldest of them – Rhiwallon – that he must become a man of medicine and a benefactor to mankind. For centuries after that, Myddfai was famous for its physicians, all said to be descended from the Lady of the Lake.

Nevern The Celtic cross in the churchyard is more than twelve feet high. According to an old tradition, the first cuckoo to reach this part of the world each spring arrives on St Brynach's Day, 7 April. The bird's first resting-place is said to be, always, the top of Nevern's Celtic cross.

Pennant A particularly malignant witch named Mari Berllan Piter lived and operated here during the nineteenth century.

Pont yr Ysbryd Gwyn The bridge, here, was the scene of a murder at the time of the Crusades. Sir Walter Mansel, arriving to meet his lover Nest, was assassinated by orders of Nest's jealous rival Gwladys. Nest saw the murderer throw her lover's body over the parapet into the river. In her grief, Nest threw herself into the water and was drowned. A 'White Lady' has been occasionally seen here, which gives the bridge its name.

Roch The castle was built in the thirteenth century by Adam, Lord of Roch, who had been told by a witch that he would die from the bite of an adder. If he managed to live for the whole of a certain year without being bitten by a snake, she added, he would after that have nothing of the sort to fear. Adam lived on the top floor of his snake-proof refuge for almost the year. On the last night of this period of self-discipline, which was bitterly cold, a basket of firewood was taken up to the castle's top floor. It contained an adder. As Adam started to throw logs on to his fire, he received the fatal bite.

St David's St Non's Well, about a mile from this small city, was used for centuries for healing purposes. It was respected, too, as a wishing-well of peculiar effectiveness.

St Dogmael's At Carreg y Fendith, by the River Teifi, in the Middle Ages, the river's fish used to be blessed by the local monks at the start of each fishing season. Efforts have been made in this century to revive the custom.

The little chapel at St Govan's Head

St Govan's Head   The small chapel of St Govan here may be – at least in part – as much as fourteen hundred years old. To reach the chapel, one has to use a long stone stair. It is said to be impossible for anyone to count these steps accurately, because a different total will be reached every time.

Inside the chapel, there is a narrow cleft in the rock which (according to tradition) first opened miraculously when St Govan needed to hide from his enemies. People still stand in this cleft, facing the wall, and wish, believing that their wishes will be granted.

Hidden in a nearby rock, there is said to be a bell that was once stolen from the chapel by pirates. When the rock is banged, the bell is supposed to ring.

Below the chapel there is a well used for centuries for healing purposes. It was thought to be particularly effective for treating diseases of the eye.

Strata Florida   The site of this abbey, dissolved and demolished during the Reformation, is said to be visited at Christmas by the shade of a monk.

Tre Taliesin   On a lonely hillside near Talybont there is a cairn which is supposed to mark the burial-place of the bard Taliesin, who died in the sixth century. Taliesin is said to have been the son of the witch Ceridwen, who threw her new baby into the sea in a coracle. The child survived, and the coracle was washed ashore near Borth.

Yspytty Ystwyth   The well-known wizard Sir Dafydd Llwyd is said to be buried here, under the churchyard wall. His friends chose this place in order to cheat the Devil, who claimed the right to take possession of Sir Dafydd's soul.

Further reading

Davies, J. C., *Folklore of West and Mid-Wales*, The Welsh Gazette, Aberystwyth, 1911.
Owen, T. M., *Welsh Folk Customs*, National Museum of Wales, Cardiff, 1974.

Further information from
The Area Librarian, Public Library, St Peter's Street, Carmarthen,
  SA31 1LN.

Gwent

Abergavenny Ysgyryd Fawr, or 'The Skirrid Mountain', once
had on its summit a small chapel dedicated to St Michael. The
mountain gained over the centuries a reputation for being
especially holy, and local people used to take soil from it to their
own land, to improve their crops or to eradicate agricultural
disease or misfortune.

Caerleon Here (as at so many other places) there is said to be a
cave in which King Arthur and his knights are sleeping.

Chepstow There is a cave in the limestone cliff below Chepstow
Castle which has also been said to be the temporary resting-place
of King Arthur and his knights.
  St Tewdric's Well, not far from Chepstow, is associated with a
King of Gwent and Glamorgan who was mortally wounded near
Tintern, around the year 470, in a battle against the pagan
Saxons. Tewdric's followers were taking him on a cart drawn by
two stags towards the Severn Estuary, hoping that they would be
able to bury him on the sacred island of Flat Holme. When they
reached this spot, clear water started to flow miraculously from
the ground, and they were able to wash the king's wounds.

Clydach High above the Clydach Gorge there is an upright
limestone pillar known as 'The Lonely Shepherd'. According
to a local tradition, the stone was once a shepherd who was
exceptionally unkind to his wife. At last, she was driven to
commit suicide by drowning herself in the River Usk. The
shepherd, for his sins, was then turned into stone. Each
Midsummer Night since then he has been impelled to go down to

the river to look for his wife. He goes back to his place on the mountain just before dawn.

Near the Drum and Monkey Inn, in the Clydach Gorge, a subway and steps lead to the Devil's Bridge. Below this, there is a spectacular waterfall, and below this, again, there is a deep pool known as 'Pwll y Cwn' ('The Pool of Dogs'). In its waters, a mischievous sprite called a 'Pwca' was in earlier centuries thought to reside.

Grosmont   The notorious wizard Jack O'Kent is believed to be buried under one of the walls of Grosmont Church – a location chosen so that the Devil would be cheated. In return for giving Jack supernatural powers during his lifetime, the Devil was promised that he could have Jack's body and soul, after the wizard's decease, whether he was buried in church or outside.

Llangybi   St Cybi's Stone, standing upright in a flat field near the river, is said to mark the spot where this peripatetic holy man started his first mission, some time in the sixth century. The local king tried to remove the saint and his followers from his land, but he failed. Instead, he lost his sight, and his horse died. Taking pity on the king, Cybi gave him back his sight and brought the horse back to life.

Llanvihangel Rogiet   The standing stone known as 'The Devil's Quoit' is said to have been thrown over the Bristol Channel to its present position by the Devil when he was more than usually annoyed.

Michaelstone-y-Vedw   A standing stone in the grounds of Druidstone House is said to move down to the nearby river at night, and to go for a swim before returning to its usual position.

Mynyddislwyn   Powder scraped from stones found here was used, until the present century, for treating dogs suffering from rabies, and, where necessary, for treating people bitten by the dogs.

The mound known as 'Twyn Tudor' near Mynyddislwyn Church is reputed to contain buried treasure. Those seeking it are said to be driven away by alarming storms.

Newport   The cathedral church is built on Stow Hill. The hill is said to be so holy that immense trouble inevitably awaits anyone foolish enough to desecrate it. Pirates who stole the plate from one church on the site were drowned when their ship sank in a terrific storm.

Pontypool   The original name of this town was 'The Bridge of ap Hywel'. Dafydd ap Hywel is supposed to have struggled with the Devil, the loser of the contest being required to build a bridge over the river. Ap Hywel won.

Risca   The mountain called 'Twm Barlwm' is said to produce mysterious music at certain times of the year.

Severn Bridge   On a small island near this bridge are the remains of a little chapel. The building is believed to have been the retreat of a hermit called St Tecla or St Tecia, who was widely known as a healer. In the ruins, the position of the saint's holy well can be traced.

Stanton   The Buckstone, on a hilltop near this village, may once have been a Druidic altar. It used to rock impressively until a party of sightseers toppled it from its ancient resting place a little more than a century ago.

Trelleck   Three standing stones in a field near here are usually referred to as 'Harold's Stones'. Tradition says that the stones were thrown here by the famous wizard Jack o'Kent. He pitched them from the top of Ysgyryd Fawr, some twelve miles distant, when he was competing with the Devil. When the Devil saw that Jack o'Kent could throw further than he could, he resigned the match and made himself scarce. (See also **Grosmont**, **Gwent**, above.)

Wilcrick   A wishing well here is still visited.

Further information from
The Bibliographical Officer, The County Library Headquarters,
    County Hall, Cwmbran, Gwent, NP44 2XL.

Gwynedd

Aberdaron   Richard Robert Jones, born in a cottage near here in
1780, became known throughout Wales as 'Dic Aberdaron'. He
was widely respected for his ability to call up obedient demons
from the Underworld. Having conjured them up, he was said to
be good at making them perform humdrum agricultural tasks.

Abersoch   On the site of the mansion Castellmarch, near here,
one of King Arthur's warriors named 'March Amheirchion' had
his stronghold, or so it has traditionally been held. Unfortunately
for March Amheirchion, he was born with a horse's ears – a
liability he tried to keep secret by murdering every barber who
came to trim his beard, and every other person who, by
mischance, learned of his deformity. He buried the bodies of his
victims in a nearby marsh, from which grew a large clump of
reeds. One day, someone made a pipe from one of these reeds.
When the pipe was played, the only sounds it would produce
seemed to say 'March Amheirchion has horse's ears'. At that,
March Amheirchion gave up trying to keep his ears secret, and let
his barbers live.

Bala   The lake – 'Llyn Tegid' – is one of several in Britain reputed
to contain a submerged town. It is also said to be the watery grave
of an eighteenth-century harpist who sold his soul to the Devil,

and who disappeared into the depths leaving behind himself a cloud of black smoke.

Bardsey   The island – 'Ynys Enlli' – two miles from the end of the Lleyn Peninsula was for centuries an important place of pilgrimage and it is sometimes said that as many as twenty thousand monks have been buried here. Some of them, it is said, still wander occasionally by the island's twilit shores.

Barmouth   The causeway Sarn Badrig runs out from the coast near here towards the reputedly submerged land of Cantre'r Gwaelod.

Beddgelert   The so-called 'grave' of Gelert, faithful hound of Llywelyn the Great, attracts thousands of visitors each year, but the romantic story of Gelert, his impulsive master, and the wolf has only in recent centuries been linked with this little town.

Clynnog Fawr   At least six North Wales churches are dedicated to St Beuno, who lived in the sixth century, and is said to have been second only in godliness and power to St David. Beuno's miracle-working shrine here was for centuries visited by pilgrims from all over Wales. In the present church at Clynnog Fawr there is an old oak strong-box, made from a single piece of wood. Until recently, the farmers of Clynnog Fawr would drive into the churchyard on Trinity Sunday all their lambs and calves that had been born with the distinctive 'Nod Beuno' or 'Beuno's slit' in their ears. The beasts would be sold, and the proceeds put into the chest for the benefit of the local monastic community and, later, for the church.

Conwy   The estuary of the river is said to have been favoured, in the distant past, by mermaids. A little way upstream, anglers find sparlings or 'brwyniad' – small fish said to have been brought into existence miraculously or magically by St Brigid, who, in a famine, threw handfuls of the local rushes into the water. Immediately, the rushes turned into the much-needed food.

Criccieth A 'Black Cave' near this seaside town is believed to be haunted by two musicians who, long ago, were tempted by fairies to enter it and were never seen again. Faint echoes of their music apparently linger on.

Dwygyfylchi Three boulders near here – one red, one white and one slate-coloured – are said to have been women turned into stones for their irreverent behaviour on the Sabbath.

Ffestiniog High on the moors near here is a small lake known as 'The Maidens' Lake' or 'Llyn y Morwynion'. Several reasons have been advanced for this name. The most popular suggests that on its shores some local men who had been to the Vale of Clwyd on a girl-stealing expedition were overtaken by the angry Clwydians and massacred. The girls, who had preferred their abductors, then plunged into the lake and drowned. Their ghosts are believed to come out of the water sometimes, in the early morning, to comb their spectral hair.

Llanbabo (Anglesey) Near the River Alaw, some stones have been said since 1722, if not before, to mark the grave of Branwen, daughter of Llyr, King of the Island of the Mighty. Branwen, heroine of the fourteenth-century epic *The Mabinogion*, had a brother Bran who owned a singular treasure – a cauldron that would restore the dead to life.

Llanbedr The site of the church here is said to have been changed at the behest of the Devil or some other supernatural being.

Llanddona (Anglesey) This was the home for centuries of a number of notorious witches, whose powers were said to pass successively, by right of birth, from mother to daughter. Members of the group relied on their evil reputations for blackmailing potential victims, and did very well out of it.

Llanddwyn (Anglesey) On this small island there are the remains of an old church, dedicated to St Dwynwen, and a mysterious well. St Dwynwen became the patron saint of Welsh lovers sometime in the fifth century when, after a disastrously frustrating affair with a local prince, she prayed that God would, thereafter, grant all requests that she might make on behalf of those truly in love.

Llandecwyn There are stones here said to be magical. They are on the grave of an alleged witch.

Llandwrog From the farm called 'Garth Dorwen', a servant is said to have been spirited away by fairies.

Llandyfrydog (Anglesey) A standing stone near here could be mistaken, in twilight, for a man with a pack on his back. It is known locally as 'The Robber's Stone' (Carreg y Lleidr). The Rev. John Skinner reported in 1802 that the country people around believed that it was a thief who had stolen some books from a nearby church and for his temerity had been petrified.

Llangwyfan (Anglesey) A cave here is reputed to contain buried treasure. Supernatural guardians prevent any human from digging it up.

Maentwrog The remote site known now as 'Tomen-y-Mur' has been, successively, a Roman fort and a Norman stronghold. At some stage in its long history, Tomen-y-Mur became associated with Lleu, the legendary hero who could only be killed by magical means. After the secret of his immunity had been found out, a poisoned spear that had been a year in the making proved too much for Lleu.

Nant Gwynant The hill known as 'Dinas Emrys', capped with an Iron Age fort, featured in the writings of Nennius (working in the eighth and ninth centuries). According to Nennius, the British tyrant Vortigern tried to build a castle here, but each night the materials were mysteriously dispersed. Vortigern's magicians told him that his stronghold would only be successfully completed if he first sprinkled its foundations with the blood of a boy born of a virgin. A boy answering to that description was found, and brought to Vortigern. The boy said that beneath the foundations there was a hidden lake which made it impossible to build the castle. In the lake, there would be found a tent containing two dragons, one red, the other white. All turned out exactly as the boy had foretold. The dragons, released, started to fight, and the red dragon (symbolising the Welsh) eventually drove the white dragon (the Saxons) from the tent (Britain). The boy ('Emrys') then took command of the citadel. When the story was retold by Geoffrey of Monmouth in the twelfth century, Geoffrey gave the prodigious boy the more evocative name of 'Merlin'.

Nefyn A phantom coach is said to have been seen near here, foretelling the imminent death of the unfortunate woman who got in its way.

Penmaenmawr A standing stone here, known as the 'Deity Stone', is said to bend its head if anyone blasphemes in its immediate locality.

Penmynydd (Anglesey) The old house called 'Penhesgyn' was once threatened by a vicious serpent which – according to an ancient prophecy – would kill the heir to the dwelling and land. To save him from this awful fate, the heir was sent away to England. While he was 'abroad' the serpent approached Penhesgyn. There, a resourceful local lad had had a deep pit dug, and over this he had placed a brightly polished brass pan. The serpent, seeing its own reflection in the brass, and believing this to be a rival, started to fight it. The local lad let the serpent tire itself out, and then killed it. Feeling safe after that, the heir returned to Penhesgyn and scornfully aimed a kick at the head of the lifeless serpent. One of the dead reptile's fangs, still capable of injecting poison, penetrated the rash man's foot and the heir succumbed, exactly as had been foretold.

Snowdonia It is said of Llyn Idwal, the mysterious lake, that no bird will ever cross it.

Trefdraeth (Anglesey) The happily-married harpist Einion, son of Gwalchmai, who lived during the thirteenth century at the house called 'Trefeilir', is said to have been lured away from it by a demon, and to have been kept spellbound for years. Eventually, after many adventures, Einion managed by magical means to make his way back to Trefeilir. There, he found that his devoted wife Angharad had been approached by the demon – disguised as a wealthy and handsome man – and had been persuaded that her husband had died some years before. To his dismay, Einion discovered that Angharad was about to marry the plausible stranger. So he played on his harp a melody of which Angharad had been, in the past, particularly fond. As soon as she heard it, Angharad knew that her rightful husband had returned. The demon, thwarted, became ugly again, and disappeared for ever.

Further reading
Barber, Chris, *Mysterious Wales*, Granada, 1982.
Roberts, Hilda E., *Legends and Folk-lore of North Wales*, Collins' Clear Type Press, 1931.

Further information from
The Area Librarian, Arfon/Dwyfor Area Library, Pavilion Road, Caernarfon, Gwynedd, LL55 1AS.

Mid Glamorgan

Caerphilly The castle – the second largest in Britain – is said to be haunted by two ghosts: a phantom moat witch (in Welsh, 'Gwrach y Rhibyn') and, haunting the ramparts, the shade of Princess Alice, wife of Gilbert de Clare, Norman overlord of the district.

Ewenny   The priory that at one time stood here was then one of the most important fortified monastic settlements in Britain. Some surviving parts of the priory are, at times, open to the public. They are said to be haunted by two ghosts: a phantom child in blue, and – appropriately – a shadowy monk.

Gilfach Fargoed   The Rhymney Valley was once full of happy fairies. Then a cruel giant came to live in the valley and started to eat them. At last, a fairy lad decided that the giant should be killed. Being able (like all fairies) to speak the language of the birds, he made a plan with a wise owl. The owl made a bow and arrows from the branches of an apple tree and shot the giant as he slept. Other fairies then gathered, to burn the hated tyrant's body. The heat of the blaze was sufficient to set fire to the ground. This is said to have indicated the presence of coal, which has since been of great economic importance to the Rhymney Valley.

Ogmore   The ruins of the Norman castle near the mouth of the river here are said to have treasure buried somewhere inside them. The hoard is guarded by the ghost of a lady in white ('Y Ladi Wen').

Rhondda   Llyn Fawr, the lake to the north of the Rhondda Valley, is said to be lived in by a shy mermaid-like figure. She emerges from the water in the early morning to comb her long golden hair. If anyone startles her, she slips back into the lake again and disappears.

Sker   Remote Sker House, near Sker Point, some three miles west of Porthcawl, is said to have been haunted by a variety of ghosts. One legend tells of 'The Maid of Sker', a girl who fell in love with a local carpenter. Because her father disapproved of the match, she was locked up in a wing of the house. Then she was forced into marriage with a gentleman from Neath, and is reputed to have died shortly afterwards from a broken heart. There have been ghostly white-robed monks at Sker, too:

reminders of the monks of Margam Abbey who used to use this house as their grange.

Further reading
Felstead, Richard, *Tales of the Rhymney Valley*, Rhymney Valley District Council, Hengoed, Mid Glamorgan, 1986.
Morgan, Alun, *Legends of Porthcawl and the Glamorgan Coast*, D. Brown and Sons, 1974.

Further information from
The County Librarian, Mid Glamorgan County Library, Coed Parc, Bridgend, CF31 4BA.

Powys

Brecon Beacons   High in these mountains, near the lake called 'Llyn Cwm Llwch', there was once a door in a rock which – local people said – opened annually to give human beings access for a day to fairyland. The privilege was withdrawn when one of the fairies' guests took away a flower.

Builth Wells   The stones that make up a cairn on the mountain Corngafallt, near here, were said by Nennius, in the ninth century, to have been collected by King Arthur, after he had been hunting the great boar Troynt. One stone is said to bear the impression of the paw of Arthur's hound Cabal. If the stone is taken away, it will always return, however far it is carried.

Cilmery   By the River Irfon here there is a stone pillar that commemorates the death in 1282 of Llywelyn ap Gruffydd, last of the native Princes of Wales. It is said that broom used to grow where Llywelyn was killed, but since his death no broom has flourished near this spot.

Crickhowell   An upright stone by the River Usk looks like a big fish standing on its tail. Local people say that each Midsummer Eve the stone dives into the water and goes for a swim.

Hyssington   Beneath the doorstep of the local church there is supposed to be buried a boot. In the boot there is a tyrannical local squire. By magic, administered by one of his victims, the tyrant was changed into a bull. The bull was as fierce as the squire had been, but it was rendered powerless and reduced in size by the local clergyman, who preached and prayed over the angry beast until the problem became manageable.

Llanbedr Painscastle   A castle here was in the twelfth century the principal stronghold of the hated Norman overlord William de Breos, who, with his forces, is said to have killed three thousand Welshmen in a single fight. De Breos' wife Maud was as terrifying as her husband. She was almost certainly a witch, and is principally remembered today by one extraordinary feat: she is said to have built Hay Castle in a single night. (See also **Llowes**, **Powys**.)

Llandeilo Graban   The last dragon to terrorise this part of the world is said to have slept every night on the tower of Llandeilo Graban church. The beast was eventually dealt with by a clever ploughboy seeking a reward. The lad made a dummy man out of a large log of oak and, aided by the local blacksmith, fitted the dummy with numerous barbed iron hooks. When the dragon attacked the dummy, it was grievously wounded and bled quickly to death.

Llanfair Caereinion   A troublesome local squire is said to have been turned by a magician into a fly. This fly is believed to have been put into a bottle. A bottle reputed to contain the fly is still carefully preserved in the district.

Llangorse Lake ('Llyn Syfaddan')

Llanfyllin Here, too, a troublesome spirit is said to have been changed, during the eighteenth century, into a fly. This fly is believed to have been put into a box. The box was then buried in a field that is still called (in Welsh) 'The Meadow of Trouble'.

Llangorse Llangorse Lake, or 'Llyn Syfaddan', is said to contain in its waters a submerged town. When the waters are troubled, the sound of church bells can be heard, or so it is claimed. The waters of the lake are also said to change colour frequently, probably for supernatural reasons. Giraldus Cambrensis, who visited the lake in the twelfth century, reported that sometimes the waters of the lake miraculously assumed a greenish hue; sometimes they appeared to be tinged with red, 'not universally, but as if blood flowed partially through certain veins and small channels'.

Llangurig 'White' witches living in Llangurig and around have for centuries been respected and consulted whenever farm animals have seemed to be suffering from the attentions of 'black' witches.

Llowes A decorated Celtic stone cross now in Llowes Church is said to have been thrown over the Wye by the witch Maud de Breos (See **Llanbedr Painscastle**, **Powys**, above.) According to some accounts, Maud at first failed to notice this stone when it was in her shoe. When it began to trouble her, she picked it out and lobbed it towards Llowes.

New Radnor Four standing stones a little way to the east of the town are said to respond to the bells of the local church. When they hear the bells, the stones are believed to go to a nearby pool to drink.

Oswestry The Llynclys Pool, near here, is believed to have in its waters a submerged palace, with all its occupants.

Trefeglwys Fairies are alleged to have stolen twin babies from a couple who once lived in this district. In their place, the wee folk left the traditional 'changelings'. The theft was discovered, and the human infants were restored.

Further reading
Coleman, S. J., *The Legendary Lore of Montgomeryshire*, The
    Folklore Academy, Douglas, Isle of Man, 1956.
Williams, A. J. Bailey, *The Enchanted Wood*, The Montgomeryshire
    Printing Co Ltd, Newtown, 1947.

Further information from
The Local History Librarian, County Library Headquarters,
    Cefnllys Road, Llandrindod Wells, Powys, LD1 5LD.
The Area Librarian, Area Library, Park Lane, Newtown, Powys,
    SY16 1EJ.

South Glamorgan

Llantrisant This was the home of the eccentric Dr William Price (1800–93). Well known as a physician and surgeon, Dr Price also claimed that he was an Arch-Druid. Scorning all orthodox religions, he used to perform strange mystical rites on the rocking stone at Pontypridd. He would dress usually in a white tunic, covering a scarlet waistcoat, while his trousers were of green cloth. On his head he wore a large fox skin. He was indicted at Cardiff Assizes in 1884, before Mr Justice Stephens, accused of having attempted to cremate the body of his infant son Iesu Grist. As a result of this sensational trial, the legality of cremation was established.

Llantwit Major There is a stone pillar by the north wall of the old church here. It has been said to have been used by the Druids as a sacrificial table. The straight, vertical channel at the back of the stone may have been carved to carry the blood of the Druids' victims to where it was needed.

Penmark The name of this place, in its Welsh form, means 'Horse's Head'. This recalls the old belief that a horse carrying messages from North Wales to King Arthur's court in Somerset fell at the place now named 'Cefn March' in Dyfed, and lost its head. The head travelled on without the remainder of the horse, until it finally came to rest, here.

St Donats The Castle is said to resound, occasionally, to the groans of a ghost in mourning. Some people believe that the ghost is lamenting the death, in the eighteenth century, of a man named Stradling. On his death, the Castle passed out of the possession of the Stradling family.

St Fagans The Welsh Folk Museum here contains many exhibits with magical connotations.

St Lythans The noteworthy cromlech in this parish is said to have certain magical properties. On Midsummer Eve, the capstone is said to rotate three times, and at Hallowe'en the stones are supposed to make wishes come true. The field in which the cromlech stands is called the 'Accursed Field', and is clearly less fertile than most others.

St Nicholas The standing stones on the Dyffryn estate are said to have exerted evil influences since the days of the Druids. It is believed to be unsafe to sleep too near these stones on certain nights – such as the eve of May Day – when supernatural forces are normally (or abnormally) unleashed. Those rash enough to do so are liable to lose their lives, or, at least, their wits.

Tongwynlais The well known as 'Taff's', or 'Fynnon Taf', was famous for the treatment of rheumatism and comparable disorders until quite late in the nineteenth century. Patients had to queue up for hours before they could be immersed in its malodorous waters.

There has been a stronghold of some kind on the site of the Victorian Castell Coch (the 'Red Castle') since the twelfth century, if not even earlier. There is said to be a secret subterranean passage which leads from the vaults beneath the present building to Cardiff Castle. Near the entrance to this tunnel there is a chamber that contains the treasure of Ifor Bach, lord of the locality when the twelfth-century castle was built. Guarding the treasure, there are two or three enormous and savage eagles. These birds have always (to this date) managed to repulse with their sharp beaks and talons persons stupid enough to seek for Ifor's concealed wealth.

Further reading
The Dictionary of Welsh Biography down to 1940, the Hon. Soc. of
   Cymmrodorion, London, 1959.

Further information from
The Reference Librarian, The Central Library, The Hayes,
   Cardiff, CF1 2QU.

West Glamorgan

Cefn Bryn   The massive capstone on the ancient burial chamber here is usually known as 'Arthur's Stone'. It is believed to have been thrown to its present location, from a spot seven miles away, by King Arthur, who was troubled by a 'pebble' in his shoe, and found this.

   People from the Swansea area who believe in magic have been drawn in considerable numbers, over the centuries, to this 'Arthur's Stone'. Girls wishing to test the faithfulness of their lovers have been known to crawl at night round the stone and its supporting complex at least three times, on their hands and knees, willing their young men to appear. (If the young men have failed to turn up, that has been taken as a sure sign of the swains' ineligibility as future husbands.) Others, who have wanted to express some wish effectively, have held in the palms of their hands water from the spring 'Ffynnon Fawr' that is associated with Arthur's Stone, and have spoken aloud their requests. The ghost of King Arthur, clad in shining armour, is said to have appeared here from time to time, and to have been reliably identified.

Glyn-Neath King Arthur is said to be sleeping, with his Knights of the Round Table, in the Craig y Ddinas Cave near here.

Llangyfelach The church and its tower, here, are separated. According to a local story, the Devil was envious of St Cyfelach and tried to make off with the tower of his church. The saint foiled the Evil One before the Devil had gone more than a few feet.

Penmaen The destruction of Pennard Castle, now reduced to insignificant ruins, is blamed, by tradition, on the fairies. When the noble Rhys ap Iestyn, who lived in the castle, gave a lavish feast to celebrate his wedding, the wee folk tried to join in with a dance of their own. Rhys, who had drunk deeply, told his men to drive them away. The fairies retaliated by sending a tremendous sandstorm.

Port Talbot The Morfa Colliery, near here, was the scene in 1890 of a terrible disaster. A subterranean explosion of the sort only too common at that time killed more than eighty miners. The death roll would have been much higher if those in the district had not been warned, in advance, by the appearance of ghostly hounds, phantom funeral processions, and other uncanny manifestations. These persuaded a good proportion of the workers not to go underground on the fatal day.

Rhosili Remote Paviland Cave, between here and Port Eynon, is said to be haunted by the ghost of a woman who once entered the cave, looking for treasure, and was then fatally trapped in it by a sudden and terrifying storm.

St Nicholas   The Dusty Forge Inn, near here, was once really a forge. The Devil is supposed to have visited it one night, when the blacksmith was away, intending to make for his own cloven feet a pair of iron shoes. He was frustrated by the blacksmith's wife, who went on tiptoe to her henhouse and woke her birds. The crowing of the cocks disturbed the Devil. He fled, leaving an unfinished shoe on the anvil.

Vale of Neath   This has the reputation of being a favourite haunt of fairies and other supernatural beings.

Ystradgynlais   On the summit of Mynydd y Drum, a little to the east of the town, there is a cairn known as 'Y Garn Goch'. Somewhere under the reddish stones gold is said to be buried, but the treasure is protected by violent demons which have so far driven away all the mortals brave enough to attempt to reach it.

Further reading
Rees, David, *A Gower Anthology*, Christopher Davies, 1977.

Further information from
The County Librarian, West Glamorgan House, 12 Orchard Street, Swansea, SA1 3SG.

Scotland

Borders

Auchencrow   Nearly every parish in this region has tales of witches, or so-called witches. To itemise them would require several books. In the seventeenth century, Auchencrow's witches were particularly notorious.

Carterhaugh   This has a real claim to be a magical place. Its original name was 'Catkemach'. This is likely to have been derived from the Gaelic 'Cathair'. This, at the time of the Gaelic intrusion, would have been translated as 'A Fairy Knoll'. There is an old ballad based on the story of a Lady Janet, daughter of the Earl of March, who met Tamlane, a local bogey, at Carterhaugh and found that he was her childhood friend, a son of Randolph, Earl Murray, who had been stolen by the Fairy Queen. She freed the fairies' prisoner, and married him.

Cranshaws   The stronghold known as 'Cranshaws Tower' was once the home of a grumpy old brownie who for years made himself useful by threshing the corn on the farm. This continued until some human tactlessly observed that the corn had not been tidily stacked in the barn. The brownie, deeply offended, took all the corn to a stream about two miles from Cranshaws and tipped it into the water. After that, the brownie was never seen again at Cranshaws.

Drumelzier   The magician Merlin is said to be buried near here. The grave is believed to be close to the spot where Pausail Burn joins the River Tweed.

Dryburgh   At one time Dryburgh was a Druid's grove, or so it is believed. In more recent centuries, a dark damp vault in the ruins of the Abbey became the home of a woman who had lost her lover in the 1745 Rebellion. She vowed that she would never see the sun again until her lover returned. When she was told that he had been killed, she refused to emerge, except at night. Then, she told people living around, her vault was tidied for her by her familiar 'Fatlips' – a little being who wore heavy iron shoes. He used these for trampling flat the clay floor of the cell.

Earlston This is said to have been the home, during the thirteenth century, of Thomas the Rhymer ('of Ercildoun', otherwise Earlstown). Noted during his lifetime as a prophet, Thomas gained a posthumous reputation as a wizard, and several witches arraigned during later centuries claimed that they owed their magical powers to his influence.

Edin's Hall This Iron Age hill fort near Duns has been said by some romantic commentators to have been the home, long ago, of Red Etin, a three-headed giant.

Ednam The burial-mound a mile or so to the west of this place has been variously called 'The Piper's Grave', 'Picts' Knowe', 'The Bogey Plantin'' and 'The Mount'. It is said to be haunted by the ghost of Thor Longus, the founder of the village. According to another tale, it proved fatal to a piper, who entered the mound to study the music of the wee folk he thought were living in it. He failed to take with him a protective talisman, and that was the end of him.

Eildon Hills James Hogg, the 'Ettrick Shepherd', claimed in 1822 that the Eildon Hills were once one large peak. The peak was split into three by a devil, he wrote, and the devil was commanded to do so by the wizard Michael Scot. The hills recall a variety of old traditions: King Arthur and his knights are said to be asleep within them; the 'Lucken Hare', a small mound near the foot of the Western Eildon, is said to have been the meeting-place of witches and warlocks; at another place at the foot of the Western Eildon a witch was burned, and since then no grass has ever grown on the spot. Somewhere below the hills, too, Thomas the

Rhymer (see **Earlston**, **Borders**, above) is said to have met the Queen of the Fairies, who took him with her to Fairyland.

Ettrick Water   Sir Walter Scott recorded an old belief that the banks of Ettrick Water were haunted by a malicious sprite called 'Shellycoat'.

Falsehope   A hill near here is called the 'Witchie Hill'. A bitter duel is said to have been fought here between the wizard Michael Scot and the Witch of Falsehope.

Fairy Dean   The River Allen, or Ellwynd, flowing through this glen is supposedly favoured by fairies for their midnight feasts. People peering into its waters, particularly after a flood, are believed to be able to see shapes of cups, plates and other utensils.

Hermitage Castle   This stronghold, built in the thirteenth century to protect the western approach to Scotland and now in ruins, has an evil reputation. One of its early owners – William, Lord Soulis, Warden of the Scottish Marches – was so wicked that nobody doubted that he was a warlock. To protect himself against harm, Soulis was said to keep a familiar spirit called 'Redcap Sly'. (The name indicates one of the less attractive habits of this malevolent goblin, and others of its kind: it was so called because it used to drain its victims' blood into their caps while they were asleep.) The shell of the castle was long thought to be haunted by the ghostly Redcap. Soulis, who had unashamedly kidnapped the young Laird of Branxholm, met his end when he was wrapped by Branxholm's men in a sheet of lead and boiled to death.

Holdean Mill   Here a miller is said to have been awakened by 'little people' playing in the ashes of his kiln fire.

Linton Sir Walter Scott was able to publish an old rhyme about

> . . . The wode laird of Lariestoun . . .

who

> . . . Slew the wode worm of Wormistoune . . .

He is said to have copied it from an inscription near a stone carving that he had seen over the door of Linton's old parish church. The sculpture shows a knight with a falcon on his arm attacking, with his lance, one of two dragons, or 'worms'. The Wormiston worm was said to have its den in a hollow piece of ground a mile to the south-east of Linton Church. It used to destroy both men and beasts that came in its way. Several attempts were made to kill it, by shooting of arrows and throwing of darts, but nobody dared approach near enough to use a sword or lance. Eventually, a John Somerville undertook to kill it. When the dragon put its head and part of its body outside its den at first light of morning, Somerville rode his horse hard at it. At the point of his lance, he had fixed some pieces of bog-turf that he had soaked with pitch and other inflammable materials. He thrust the blazing weapon directly into the dragon's mouth, so that it went down the beast's throat into its belly, giving it a deadly wound. For this action, he was given a knighthood. Those who look from Linton Church towards 'Wormiston' (Linton Hill) are said to be able to see the marks of the dragon's coils.

Melrose Abbey At Melrose Abbey, one can see the reputed grave of Michael Scot, probably the leading scholar of western Europe in the early thirteenth century. Scot was a great student of magic, though he did not appear to differentiate between it and astrology, which also fascinated him. Many fanciful stories were woven about Scot and his times, long after his death; in some accounts of his life, he was credited with the ability to fly by magical means. In his *Superstitions of the Highlands and Islands of Scotland*, published in 1900, John Gregorson Campbell claimed that once when Scot wanted to visit Rome, he rode on a fairy horse that travelled faster than the wind. The Pope was astonished to see snow still on Scot's bonnet.

Minchmoor   Fairies are said to live by the spring called 'The Cheese Well' on top of the Minchmoor near Traquair. The well was given this name because people passing it used to leave gifts of cheese for the Little People.

Oakwood   Michael Scot, the Scottish wizard of the early thirteenth century (see **Melrose Abbey**, **Borders**, above) has been said by at least one writer to have lived at Oakwood Tower on Ettrick Water.

Preston   Near here are the remains of the ancient fortress usually known as 'Edin's Hall' (q.v., above).

Yarrow   One of the local witches here is said to have ridden each night, as if he were her horse, a boy apprenticed to the town's blacksmith. The boy's older brother outwitted the witch. He took his brother's place one night, and managed by magic to force the witch into submission. Having the hag at his mercy, he nailed horseshoes to each of her hands and feet.

Further reading
Lochhead, Marion, *Magic and Witchcraft of the Borders*, Robert Hale, 1984.

Further information from
The Regional Librarian, Borders Regional Library Headquarters, St Mary's Mill, Selkirk, TD7 5EW.

Central

Aberfoyle   Robert Kirk, Presbyterian Minister of this town
during the late seventeenth century, was a serious scholar, and
much preoccupied with fairies and their doings. The members of
his congregation, less erudite than he, regarded his researches
into the supernatural as dangerous meddling. When the Minister
was found unconscious one morning by Aberfoyle's Fairy Hill,
the locals decided that he had been abducted by fairies and was
hidden in their hill. The apparently senseless body being carried
back to his home was a 'stock', or image left by the fairies in the
likeness of the abducted person.

Menstrie   This seems to have been regarded in past centuries as
a particularly favoured haunt of fairies. They are said to have
carried away with them – on different occasions – the Black Laird
of Dunblane and the bonny wife of an honest Menstrie miller.
Both abductees managed successfully to escape.

Touch Hills   A poor woman of this place who was afflicted with
a drunken and good-for-nothing husband is said to have been
carried away by the fairies to their palace, where she was able
to live like a queen. This happy outcome of her troubles was
reported in *The Scottish Journal of Topography*, published in 1848.

Further reading
Fergusson, R. Menzies, *The Ochil Fairy Tales*, first published 1912;
    reprinted by Clackmannan District Library, 1985.

Further information from
The Librarian, The Central Regional Council School Library
    Service, Old High School, Academy Road, Stirling, FK8 1DG.

Dumfries and Galloway

Anwoth Cardoness Castle, here, is said to have become a ruin through a curse placed on the family that once occupied it. Three successive lairds went bankrupt. The fourth gave a party on the frozen Black Loch, which is not far away. The feast was held on the Sabbath. The ice broke, and the Laird, his family, and all their servants were drowned.

Closeburn The grounds of the Castle, built in the fourteenth century, used to be visited regularly by a pair of swans, and the birds were regarded as bringers of good fortune. Then Robert Kirkpatrick, the young heir, shot one of the swans in an attempt to find out if these birds really do sing when they are about to die. After that, the reappearance of a single swan by the Castle came to be relied on as an omen of death. Usually it would be the head of the family that was fated to die in the near future.

Crawick The mill here was once the home of a notorious witch.

Glasserton St Medana's Well, on the shores of Monreith Bay, has been visited for centuries by those suffering from whooping cough. According to a local tradition, St Medana (or Modwenna) sailed here from Whithorn, using a rock as a boat. She was pursued by an importunate admirer, who refused to accept her consistent rejections. Realising that he was fascinated by the beauty of her eyes, the virtuous young woman plucked them out and threw them at his feet. Water then sprang from the ground at the spot. When Medana bathed her face, her sight is said to have been miraculously restored. The lover, by then, had departed.

Kirkmaiden Three wells in a cave about half a mile to the south of Mull Farm have been visited for centuries by those seeking infallible cures for the diseases of children. Usually the visitors would come at sunrise on the first Sunday in May. Each child to be treated would be held by one leg and immersed in the largest of the three pools. Then that leg would be submerged in the middle pool. Water from the third pool would be used for washing the patient's eyes. Finally, a small offering would be left in the cave.

Laurieston   The house 'Slogarie' some two miles north of here was once the home of a wicked laird. He and his sons are said to have come to terrible ends after they had thrown the Bible of the Laird's dead wife on a fire on a Sunday.

Lochmaben   An old woman who once lived here is reported in Cromek's *Remains of Nithsdale and Galloway Song* (1910) to have been returning home from a 'gossiping' late one evening when 'a little lovely boy, dressed in green' came to her. The boy, who was clearly a fairy who lived in the ground beneath the old woman's cottage, asked her to throw her dishwater, in future, farther from her doorstep, as 'it pits out our fire!' The old woman complied with the little boy's request, and for the rest of her life was blessed with good fortune.

Mochrum   The White Loch of Myrton, near here, used to have a reputation for curing many diseases. The patient was supposed to go to the loch on the first Sunday of February, May, August or November; to dip in it three times; and to leave some offering at the lakeside.

Moffat   The farm called 'Bodesbeck' some six miles to the north-east of Moffat is said to have once been the home of an industrious brownie. This creature worked so hard, in fact, that the farmer's prosperity became obvious to all living in the district. Then, one day, after a particularly successful harvest, the farmer thought that the brownie deserved an appropriate reward. So he left a jug of milk and a loaf of bread outside the farmhouse. The brownie was deeply offended by this gesture and stamped off in a huff. Since then, the farmers at Bodesbeck have had to do without supernatural aid.

New Abbey Cromek, in his *Remains of Nithsdale and Galloway Song*, tells of a young man of New Abbey who overheard two fairies planning to steal his wife. The young man hurried home, closed all his windows and doors and, in silence, held his wife in his arms. At midnight, footsteps were heard outside, and someone or something rapped three times on the door. The young man's cattle and horses were greatly disturbed by the visitor, and so was the young man's wife, who struggled to free herself from her silent husband's arms. At last, footsteps were heard again as the intruder departed. As soon as dawn came, the young man went outside and found, carved from moss oak, an effigy of his wife. This had clearly been intended, fairy-fashion, as a substitute for the young woman chosen for abduction.

Parton The Holy Well near the gardens of Parton House was used as a wishing-well until quite recently.

Sanquhar Between Broomfield Farm and Welltrees Meadow, here, there is a well dedicated to St Bride. On each May Day for centuries it has been customary for the maidens of Sanquhar to visit this well. Each takes with her nine smooth white stones as an offering to the saint.

Troqueer The Well of St Queran, or Jergon, on Barbush Farm, has been visited for many centuries by those seeking relief from their illnesses. When the well was cleaned out in 1870, coins dating from the reign of Elizabeth I were found.

Tynron The land round Tynron Castle is said to be haunted by a headless ghost. This may be the restless spirit of a young man from Balgarnock who wanted to marry the daughter of the Great McGachan who once lived in the castle. Her brothers, thinking that the suitor was not good enough to marry the girl, chased the unwelcome visitor away and drove him and his horse over the edge of the nearby crag. As he fell, the young man's head is said to have been knocked from his shoulders.

Further information from
The Regional Librarian, Ewart Library, Catherine Street,
    Dumfries, DG1 1JB.

Fife

Aberdour   St Fillan's Well, some thirty yards to the south-east of
the old churchyard, used to be visited by many pilgrims with
diseases of the eye, some of whom had travelled long distances.
Water from the well was reputed to be an almost certain cure for
such cases.

Auchtermuchty   The Devil is said locally to have been dismayed
by the propriety of the people of Auchtermuchty. So he disguised
himself as a Calvinist minister and came to preach in the village.
His sermon was so well received that all the members of the
congregation except one vowed that they would do whatever the
new preacher required of them. The odd man out – a senior
citizen named Robin Ruthven – lifted the preacher's black
cassock, saw the Devil's cloven feet, and raised the alarm in
(literally) the nick of time.

Culross   It used to be believed that an underground passage ran
from the Cistercian Abbey here (founded in 1217) to a secret
chamber to the north of Culross, in which a man sat in a golden
chair surrounded by treasure which he was ready and willing to
give away. A blind piper and his dog are said to have entered the
vaults at the head of the Newgate. The sound of his pipes was
heard as far as the West Kirk, a distance of some three-quarters of
a mile. Then the piping stopped. The dog later crawled out from
the entrance in Newgate without a hair on its body, and it died
soon after. On a still night, the sound of a muffled pibroch, like a
distant echo, may reputedly be heard near the site of the ancient
Monk's Well, three-quarters of a mile or so north of Culross.

Fordell   The ruins of the mill here were said to be haunted by the ghost of the miller's assistant, unjustly hanged by Cromwellian soldiers who were looking for, and unable to find, the miller.

There is a wishing well in the grounds of Fordell Castle, near Fordell House.

Kirkton of Largo   Largo Law, which is of volcanic origin, is said locally to have been formed from a rock dropped by the Devil as he flew past. At the top of the Law, there is a formation known as 'The Devil's Chair'. This has seven steps by which the Devil would have approached it. The wizard Michael Scot is said to have set his demons the task of levelling Largo Law. They had only thrown one shovelful from the top when they were called away. The cairn known as 'Norrie's Law' on the northern coast of the Firth of Forth is popularly supposed to have been formed from this shovelful.

Pittenweem   In the early eighteenth century, after a local boy said that evil spirits had been sent to torture him, the people of this place were affected by anti-witch hysteria. Suspects were imprisoned, beaten and tortured. One poor woman managed to escape from her torturers, but when the mob caught her she was stoned and then crushed to death under a door piled with heavy rocks.

Strathmiglo   John Leighton, in his *History of Fife* published in 1840, told of a brownie who used to live at Strathmiglo Castle and who would cross the River Meglo by stepping-stones each day on the way to his work at the Tower of Cash. Though this brownie was quite invisible to human eyes, people could see the work going on, and could tell when, unseen, he was helping himself to food.

West Wemyss   The Castle of Wemyss is reputedly haunted by a female ghost. She is said to be tall and thin, and to be dressed in green.

Further reading
Boucher, Robert, *The Kingdom of Fife: Its Ballads and Legends*,
   Dundee, 1899.
Simpkins, John Ewart, *Examples of Printed Folklore Concerning Fife*
   (Volume 7 of *Country Folklore*), Sidgwick and Jackson, London,
   1914.

Further information from
The Senior Librarian, Reference Department, Central Library,
   Abbot Street, Dunfermline, KY12 7NW.

Grampian

Aboyne St Munricha's Well, half a mile from Dykehead Farm,
has near it the saint's stone cross. The spirit of the well was
reputed to fetch the cross back if anyone was rash enough to
remove it.

Ben Macdui This mountain in the Cairngorms is said to be
haunted by a grey ghost (male) which is at least ten feet tall. The
ghost is reputed to have chased frightened travellers as far as the
outskirts of Braemar, a distance of approximately eleven miles.

Birse Here, belief in the magical power of May Day fires lingered
on until the middle of the nineteenth century.

Burghead The midwinter fire festival called 'Burning the Clavic'
has survived, here, into the 1980s. Glowing embers obtained
when the contents of the burning peat-filled barrel (the 'clavic')
are finally dispersed are believed to keep away evil spirits and to
bring good fortune to their possessors for the remainder of the
year.

Chapel of Garioch   A stone here, decorated with Pictish symbols, is said by some to have once been a girl named Janet of Drumdurno. When a warlock tried to rape her, Janet fled from him, and as she ran she prayed that she should be saved from his clutches. Just as the warlock caught her, Janet's prayers were answered, and she became the slab now known as 'The Maiden Stone'.

Corgarff   A boulder, here, is known as 'The Kelpie's Stone'. It is supposed to have been thrown by a frustrated water-monster at one of its intended victims after the man concerned had escaped from the kelpie's grip.
   The Bride's Well, also at Corgarff, used to be visited on the evening before their wedding by girls from miles around. With her, each girl would bring the friends who were going to act as her bridesmaids. They would bathe her feet and the upper part of her body with water from the well. This was thought to ensure that she would have a happy married life and a healthy family.

Delnabo   The lonely fastnesses of Craig Aulnic are said to have been disturbed, long ago, by turbulent goblins.

Duffus   The ruined fourteenth-century castle here was once the home of the Lord Duffus who (according to John Aubrey in his *Miscellanies*) was suddenly carried away from the surrounding fields by fairies. He was found next day in Paris, in the French King's cellar, with a silver cup in his hand. Taken before the King and questioned, Lord Duffus told how he had heard the fairies calling out 'Horse and Hattock!' – the words all fairies were supposed to use before carrying out an abduction. The King believed Lord Duffus's story, gave him the cup that had been found in his hand, and dismissed him.

Edinglassie   About a mile from here, at Hill of Dunmeth, are traces of St Walloch's Church, with, nearby, in the River Deveron, two pools called 'The Saint's Baths'. In these, people used to bathe to cure their ills, and in them, too, mothers used to wash their sickly children, in the firm belief that this would make the ailing bairns strong.

Forres   The tenth-century King Duff of Scotland is supposed to have been made sick by a coven of Forres 'haggs', who were found roasting in front of a fire a likeness of the King carried out in wax. No doubt Shakespeare had this in mind when he wrote some of the scenes in Macbeth.

Fyvie   The castle at Fyvie is said to have been cursed. In its walls, or in the River Ythan which runs through its wooded park, there were said to be three mysterious stones, possibly brought to Fyvie from some nearby religious house and having some special talismanic power. Until those three stones were found, the curse said, there would be a malison on the place. Time after time since the curse was laid, the owners of the castle have failed to produce a male heir.

A well near the site of St Paul's Chapel on the Hill of Easterton used to attract many sick people on the first Sunday in May. The pilgrims would drink from the well and would then throw a pin or a coin into it. Mothers would take their sickly children there. After making the children drink, the women would make them pass through the nearby dolmen, and under the renowned 'Shagar Stone'. The word 'shagar' means 'sick child'.

Glenbervie   St Conon's Well here was also much visited on the first Sunday in May. Those making a silent wish would throw three pins over their shoulder and into the water.

Gordonstoun   This was the home of the terrifying warlock Sir Robert Gordon, seized by the Devil and taken off to Hell in November 1704.

Hopeman   Water in the well called 'Brae Mou' to the east of Hopeman was supposed to have magical properties at Beltane (in May) and Hallowe'en (October). Mothers would bathe their children here to preserve them from the Evil Eye.

Huntly This town has been for centuries the centre of a secret society with magical undertones. Called 'The Horseman's Word', it was (and maybe still is) an organisation aimed at giving its members supernatural control over horses.

Kirkmichael Fergan's Well, high on the Cnoc Feargan above Balredan, used to be much visited by those suffering from skin diseases and running sores.

Marykirk St John's Well, in the grounds of Balmanno House, was favoured for children with rickets, and for adults with sore eyes.

Methlick The ruins of Gight Castle, three miles north of here, are said to be haunted by a ghostly piper.

Nigg People used to flock on the first Sunday of each year to St Fittack's Well, south of the ruined St Fittack's Church to the west of the Bay of Nigg. Water from the well was said to guarantee the saint's protection for the following twelve months. It was usual for pilgrims to leave beside the well some rag or strip of cloth as a symbolic offering.

Orton St Mary's Well, set in the walls of a pre-Reformation chapel about a mile to the north-east of Orton House, used to be much visited on the first Sunday in each May, and at other times. Water brought away from the well was said to be particularly effective for treating rheumatism, whooping cough, and diseases of the eye.

Portgordon Fishermen sailing from here in past centuries used to keep a keen lookout for the local merman. If they saw him, they would always turn round and head back to port.

Skene This was the home of Alexander Skene (born 1680) who went to Italy to study the Black Arts. He returned to Skene, after seven years, as a skilful and enterprising wizard. Even in bright sunlight, it was said, his body cast no kind of shadow.

Stonehaven   Fire ceremonies with ancient origins have been kept up here at Hogmanay (New Year's Eve).

Tomintoul   Grigor Willox, one of the most celebrated 'White Wizards' of the eighteenth century, used to live in Tomintoul when he was not away on his highly lucrative travels.

Further reading
McPherson, J. M., *Primitive Beliefs in the North-East of Scotland*, Longmans, Green and Co., 1929.

Further information from
The Resources Development Officer (Requests Library), Resources Centre, Belmont Street, Aberdeen, AB1 1JG.

Highland

Avoch   The water of Craigie Well, on the north shore of Munlochy Bay, is believed to be of value in combating disease, bad fairies, and witchcraft. Local people still make journeys to the well on the first Sunday in each May.

Clachnaharry   A well called by some 'Fuaran Allt an Ionnlaid' and by others 'Montrose's Well' can be found near the old tollhouse on the Muirtown road. It has been particularly favoured by people suffering from diseases of the skin, from rheumatism and from gout. Patients are expected to wash themselves in the burn close by before drinking water from the well.

Cononbridge   The River Conon, notoriously unsafe in times of flood, has several reaches where vicious water-spirits or 'kelpies' have been reported. One of the most picturesque of these danger-spots is in the woods near Conon House.

Culloden St Mary's Well, near here, is another watering-place that has been much visited early in May. It has acted as a wishing-well, and as a place of healing. Many coins have been thrown into the well, and trees nearby have been liberally decorated with rags and strips of cloth.

Dunvegan, Skye One of the most extraordinary possessions of the MacLeods of Dunvegan is a fairy flag. This tattered silk banner is said to have been brought back from the Holy Land by a crusading MacLeod, but there are other, more fanciful, accounts of its origins. There is a tradition that if the MacLeods are ever in desperate danger, they have only to unfurl the flag in battle, and they will become invincible. The flag has been used, twice, to save the principal members of the clan – once in the fifteenth century and once in the sixteenth. The magic can only be invoked three times, it is believed, so there has been no rush to unfurl the flag in recent wars.

Durness In Smoo Cave, by the sea near here, the seventeenth-century wizard Lord Reay is said to have had a brief encounter with his former tutor the Devil. The Devil and the witches who were with him escaped by blowing holes in the roof of the cave. The holes are still visible.

Glenelg There is a mound here that is said to have some connection with the Celtic goddess Bride, Queen of the Serpents. On St Brigid's Day, 1 February, snakes are believed to come out of the mound.

Inverness The medieval wizard Michael Scot is said to have made his demons build a bridge for the people of this town.

A mile to the south-west of Inverness there is a well called 'Fuaran a Chreigain Bhreac' or 'The Well of the Spotted Rock'. This used to be treated as fairies' property: any mother who had an undersized child which could have been a fairy changeling would be encouraged to leave it overnight by the well. With the child, she would leave some suitable gift for the fairies – a bowl of milk, perhaps, or a cake. On the following morning, she would expect to find her own, large, healthy child where the weakling had been.

Loch Duich   The seals seen in the loch are more or less constant reminders of the seal-maidens said to have been wooed and wed, in the past, by local fishermen.

Loch Heilen   For many centuries, this loch has had a reputation as a place of miraculous healing. Sufferers used to bathe in its waters before dawn. They would have to leave before sunrise, and would have to donate silver coins to the presiding spirit.

Loch Maree   On the island in this loch, strange rituals used to be carried out that involved the sacrifice of animals, and other pre-Christian activities.

Loch Monar   This small loch has been used over a number of centuries for healing. Patients came for treatment on the first Mondays of February, May, August and November. For the cure to be effective, the patient would have to arrive before midnight. Then the processes of dipping, drinking and coin-donating would have to be completed in time for the treated person to be out of sight of the loch before the sun rose.

Loch Ness   This sizeable loch is said to have been brought into existence by an act of carelessness. The bed of the loch was once a green and fertile glen, or so the story goes. In this glen there was a magic well which provided all the water that anyone could need. There was a condition, though – anyone drawing water from the well had to be sure to replace its cover. One day, when a woman was drawing water, she heard her baby crying. She rushed away to soothe the child, discarding the cover as she went. Before she could find and replace it, the waters of the well had started to overflow.

Sleat, Skye The waters of a well near Elgol, by Loch Scavaig, and of another at Strolamas, not far away, are believed to have some magical quality that will make childless couples fertile.

Staffin, Skye A savage and unpredictable ghost is said to have been greatly feared here, and at Trotternish. It used to murder travellers by throwing its head at them.

Storr, Skye A high stone pillar, here, was one of a pair. The two pillars are said locally to have been an old man and his old wife who went looking for a cow that had strayed. Unfortunately for them, they met some giants with magical powers, who turned the intruders into stone. The 'wife' stone has since fallen on its side.

Strathpeffer The Devil is said to wash himself and his foul-smelling clothes beneath the ground here. The theory is given substance by the local mineral springs which produce waters impregnated with both sulphur and iron. Where the waters containing these mingle, they become heavily discoloured.

Torridon This place, once so remote, has for centuries been a reputed centre of witchcraft.

Urquhart Bay Near the Temple Pier at Drumnadrochit there is a well dedicated to St Ninian. Until quite recently, the walls and trees near this well would be hung with rags and strips of cloth donated by visitors who believed that with their humble offerings they were leaving behind their troubles.

Further reading
Stewart, W. Grant, *Popular Superstitions of the Highlands of Scotland*, Constable, Edinburgh, 1823; Ward Lock, 1970 (reprint).

Further information from
The Senior Librarian (Reference), Regional Library Service, 31A
    Harbour Road, Inverness, IV1 1UA.

Lothian

Dalhousie   An old oak tree growing near Dalhousie Castle
was said to shed a branch whenever a member of the family
occupying the castle was about to die.

Edinburgh   The murder of Rizzio – Mary, Queen of Scots' Italian
secretary – in Holyroodhouse in 1566 was particularly bloody, for
he was stabbed fifty-six times. After that, his corpse was left all
night on the floor at the outer door of the Queen's apartments.
For centuries, a dark stain on the floor here was shown to visitors
as 'Rizzio's blood'. The stain could not be removed, it was said,
however often the floor was washed. A brass tablet now covers
the spot.

Leith   Richard Bovet, in his *Pandaemonium, or The Devil's Cloyster*,
published in 1684, tells of a Fairy Boy of Leith. This child of ten or
eleven, who had 'a cunning much above his years', used to act as
a drummer for the fairies. Every Thursday night the boy used to
slip away to join the members of the supernatural company in
their meeting-place under Calton Hill.

Liberton   Water from the celebrated Balm Well here was believed
in earlier centuries to be capable of curing skin diseases and even
leprosy. The well was supposed to derive its healing powers from
a drop of oil brought to Scotland in the eleventh century from the
tomb of St Catherine on Mount Sinai.

North Berwick   Witches here attempted by raising a tempest to
sink the ship in which James VI of Scotland was returning from
Norway with his bride, Anne of Denmark, in 1590. Suspects were

seized and tortured and the evidence given at their trials seems to have left James with an intense interest in, and horror of, sorcery.

Philipstoun The Binns, near here, was once the home of General Tam Dalyell, the dreaded Royalist scourge of the Covenanters during the wars that sadly affected Scotland during the seventeenth century. Dalyell's military skills were so formidable, and his cruelty so pronounced, that the Covenanters decided that he was in league with the Devil. He is said to have played cards with the Devil, too, at The Binns.

Roslin The Prentice Pillar in the fifteenth-century Roslin Chapel is said to have been carved by an apprentice while his master was in Rome, seeking advice about the right way to deal with the stone. When he returned to Roslin and found that the job had already been completed, the master was so enraged that he took a hammer and killed the apprentice.

Further information from
The Regional Information Office, Regional Chambers, Parliament
    Square, Edinburgh, EH1 1TT.

Orkney

Eynhallow This is the legendary summer home of the local sea-creatures which had mated with humans. Regarded as the holy island of Orkney, Eynhallow is believed to vanish occasionally.

Hestwall The farm of Clumly, near here, is said to have been the scene of a murder during the nineteenth century. Since then, on stormy nights, the white horse on which the murderer carried his victim's body to the sea is said to reappear.

Hoy The Dwarfie Stane on this island is a massive sandstone block in which, many hundreds of years ago, a burial chamber was cut. Local people have tended to believe that the stone, with its hole, was once the home of a giant and his wife, but Sir Walter Scott, who is thought to have visited Hoy in 1814, preferred to ascribe ownership of the stone to a 'trow' or troll.

Noltland This ruined castle on Westray was built in the sixteenth century and for a long time it was the home of members of the Balfour family. They claimed that they saw ghostly lights whenever a member of the family was born or was married. Forthcoming deaths were proclaimed by the howling of the castle's spectral hound.

Overbister This place, on Sanday, has had in its time some celebrated witches. The fingermarks of the Devil (or grooves that are claimed to be such) can be seen in the stonework of the ruined Kirk of Lady, near here.

Scapa Whalers, operating from here, are said to have had their industry spoiled by a witch to whom they had given offence.

Stenness The two celebrated stone circles near here, on Mainland, have been traditionally used by courting couples. Promises made in the circles have long been considered especially auspicious.

Swona The whirlpool known as the 'Wells of Swona' is said to have been brought into existence by a witch. She was jealous of a younger woman, and resolved to drown her. Her plans went wrong when her victim's lover tried to rescue his sweetheart, but failed. The witch, struggling to free herself from the drowning man, put the waters in a ferment.

Wyre The islands of Rousay and Stronsay are littered with large boulders. Local people say that these were the missiles used by a twelfth-century Norse giant who lived in Wyre Castle.

Yetnasteen This great stone on Rousay is said to travel to the Loch of Scockness each New Year's morning. It drinks there, and then returns to base.

Further reading
Marwick, Ernest W., *The Folklore of Orkney and Shetland*, Batsford, 1975.

Further information from
The Chief Librarian, The Orkney Library, Laing Street, Kirkwall, Orkney.

Shetland

Burra Firth Here, on Unst, giants lived – or so it is locally believed.

Esha Ness Here, on Mainland, a deep chasm is known as 'The Holes of Scraada'. The Devil was made to excavate this chasm, it is said locally, as a punishment for wrecking ships on the Ve Skerries. The groans His Satanic Majesty emitted while he dug can still be heard echoing, by those with keen ears, if they listen carefully in this ravine; or so it is said.

Fetlar The circle of low stones in this parish is known as 'The Haltadans' – otherwise, 'The Limping Dance'. The stones are popularly supposed to have been trows or trolls who used to enjoy their ungainly dances here, by moonlight, until one night they were so carried away that they went on dancing till dawn. Then, as punishment, they were turned into stones. The two stones at the centre of the circle may have been the 'trowie fiddler' and his wife. Other small groups of stones to the north-west of the Haltadans are called, locally, 'The Fiddlers' Crus', or 'The Fiddlers' Enclosures'.

Fitful Head   In an almost inaccessible cave in this rugged part of the Islands there once lived a sheep-stealing monster called 'Black Eric', or so the story goes. To get to the cave, Black Eric had to travel on a demon sea-horse. This creature went on terrorising the district long after Black Eric had been mastered by a courageous local crofter.

Foula   Hidden now, but known to have had its opening near the summit of the hill called 'Hamnafjeld', there is a vertical shaft or chimney that passes down through the rock to the level of the sea. Here, until the opening was sealed for safety reasons, lived many local trows or trolls. They protected their privacy with magical powers. Anyone new to Foula who dared to approach the hole would be sure to rue the consequences.

Lerwick   Towards the end of each January, there is a fire festival in this Mainland town. The origins of 'Up-Helly-Aa' are uncertain, but the flame-lit ceremonies may have survived, with interruptions, from the days of the Viking occupation of the Orkneys. At that time the bodies of Viking kings and chiefs were burned in great splendour while their spirits travelled to the Nordic Heaven, or 'Valhalla'.

Northmavine   Trowie Knowe, a chambered cairn in this parish on the Islands, is said to have once been inhabited by 'hill trows' – small trolls, normally dressed in grey, who left their hiding-places only by night.

Scalloway   Gallow Hill, some two miles to the north of this Mainland village, was used whenever a local witch had to be burned. Some say that traces of ashy detritus can still be found here by those ghoulish enough to search for them.

Ve Skerries   These wave-beaten rocky islets were once believed to be the occasional haunt of sea-trows – creatures that were more like human beings than the small, ugly trolls supposed to exist on

Part of the festival of Up-Helly-Aa at Lerwick, Shetland

land. The sea-trows lived normally in the depths of the ocean, but could survive the change to the upper air by clothing themselves temporarily in the skins of amphibious animals.

Further reading
Nicolson, James R., *Shetland Folklore*, Robert Hale, 1981.
Saxby, Jessie M. E., *Shetland Traditional Lore*, Grant and Murray, Edinburgh, 1932.

Further information from
The Director of Library Services, Town Hall, Lerwick, Shetland, ZE1 0HB.

Strathclyde

Alloway   Here Robert Burns was born in January 1759. From an early age, Burns was fascinated by tales of the supernatural, especially when these related to places he knew. In one of his best-loved poems, Burns tells how the farmer Tam O'Shanter saw the Devil playing bagpipes at the old Kirk of Alloway so that the local witches could dance to his Satanic tune.

Ardbeg, Islay   A standing stone about a mile to the north-east of Ardbeg is believed to mark the grave of Ila, a Danish princess. She is said to have been able to walk over the sea from Ireland to Islay as magical stepping-stones appeared most conveniently in her path.

Colmonell   A mermaid used to come out of the water near Knockdolian Castle, according to Robert Chambers in his *Popular Rhymes of Scotland*, published in 1870. For hours she would sit on a black stone by the castle, singing and combing her hair. Then

Culzean Castle

the lady of the castle, thinking that the music disturbed her baby, told her servants to smash the black stone. When the mermaid inferred, from that, that she was *persona non grata*, she laid a curse on the castle and the family that lived in it. The baby was found dead; the parents died heirless.

Creagan St Cairrell's Well, on the lower slopes of Beinn Churalain, has been visited for centuries by the sick, who used to go to it with particular enthusiasm on St Patrick's Day. Latterly, it has been recommended to all those who have had a strong desire for something so far unattainable. If such a person drank of the well's waters and left a silver coin on a little shelf on the rock beside the well, his or her wish would surely be granted, or so it was said. The priest from the chapel nearby used to collect the coins. In return, he would pray that the donor's wishes might be heard and properly dealt with.

Culzean The eighteenth-century Castle, perched on a cliff, and built on the site of much earlier strongholds, has been the setting for some strange supernatural activities. From here, for instance, one heiress is said to have been abducted by a murderous Elf-Knight. Here, too, according to another story, a small boy with a little wooden can in his hand approached the owner near the Castle Gate, and asked for some ale for his sick mother. The Laird sent him indoors to the butler, telling him to tell the butler to fill the can. The butler tried to do so, taking the ale from a cask that was about half full. Before the can was full, the cask ran dry. The butler, not wishing to open another cask, went to ask the Laird what he should do. The Laird told him to fill the can, even if that meant emptying every cask left in the cellar. Years later, when the Laird was a prisoner in France, and due to be executed, he was rescued from his dungeon by the same little boy, who appeared magically in his cell and, opening the doors, told him to 'Rise an' go!'

Finuary There is a celebrated Wishing Spring close to the boundary stone on the B849 road, not far from Finuary Manse. Before any wish can be granted, the suppliant has to keep a mouthful of water from the spring in his or her mouth while trying to squeeze through a narrow cleft in the rock. If the water is released, the wish is sure to fail.

Glasgow   The first church here is believed to have been founded by St Kentigern, later called 'St Mungo'. Many stories are told of his supernatural powers, but his reputation appears to be based on evidence as uncertain as that of the magician Merlin.

Iona, Mull   On this lonely island, many kings, princes and chiefs have been buried, their resting-place chosen principally for the sanctity of its soil, which is said to efface all sin. As a further advantage, Iona was for a long time supposed to be the only place that would survive a second Great Flood.

Mains Castle   Here, a sister of King William the Lion was strangled by her husband. Her ghost has been seen, letting her phantom lover down from a window of the tower.

Port Glasgow   Robert Chambers, in his *Popular Rhymes of Scotland*, tells of a mermaid who used to live in the Firth of Clyde not far from here. When this mermaid saw, passing her usual beat, the funeral procession of a young girl who had died of phthisis, she put her head out of the water and commented that if maidens drank nettles in March and ate mugwort flowers in May, not so many of them would go to early graves. Mugwort has been over the centuries one of the commonest herbs used in magical practice.

Tiree   This island in the Inner Hebrides was much plagued by witches in the olden days, its historians record. To get some protection from milk-stealing hags, the locals used to put balls of hair in their fresh milk on the first day of each August.

Tobermory, Mull   Here, too, witches were troublesome through several centuries. The Tobermory witches were especially proficient at raising storms at sea.

Further information from
The Hon. Librarian, E. A. Hornel Art Gallery and Library,
    Broughton House, Kirkcudbright, DG6 4JX.
Glasgow District Libraries Reference Services, The Mitchell
    Library, North Street, Glasgow, G3 7DN.

Tayside

Arbroath For nearly forty years, in the early eighteenth century,
the members of the congregation of St Vigeans Church, near
here, refused to let their ministers hold a Communion service.
They believed an old tradition that their church had been built
with stones carried by a water kelpie, and that under the fabric
there was a lake of great depth. They thought that the first time
the sacrament was dispensed the church would sink and
everyone in it would be carried down and drowned. At last, in
1736, a brave minister took the risk. The members of his
congregation watched from a safe distance. The church still
stands.

Ardtalnaig Water from the Claggan Well, near the path from
Ardtalnaig to Dunan, was believed for centuries to be good for
ailing children. The little patient had to be placed between two
stones on the brink of the well on the Eve of Beltane (1 May, Old
Style). At sunrise next morning the child would be dipped in the
well, or sprinkled with its water. As the parents left with the
child, they would throw a coin or some other gift into the well.

Broughty Ferry The people who once occupied Claypots Castle
used to have their domestic tasks done for them by an energetic
brownie, who used to work at nights and asked for no
greater reward than a bowl of cream. They lost their supernatural
servant, however, when he became disgusted with a wasteful
kitchen maid. Being by nature a perfectionist, he left the premises

for ever, calling down a curse on the castle and all its occupants as he went.

Sometimes, on 29 May, a 'White Lady' has been seen at the castle. She is supposed to have been Marion Ogilvy, the sweetheart of Cardinal Beaton. He was murdered on 29 May 1546.

Comrie High on the hill called 'Dunfillan' near here, there is a naturally formed rock seat. From this prominence, St Fillan is said to have blessed the district and all living in it. In recent centuries, people suffering from backache have gone up to sit on St Fillan's Seat. The hardiest of them have then allowed themselves to be pulled down the hill by their ankles.

Cortachy The Castle is said to be haunted by a drummer who gives warning, with his drum, when a member of the Ogilvy family is about to die.

Dunkeld Grew's Well, near here, used to be much visited on the first Saturday in each May by people who wanted to immerse their sick children in its waters at sunrise on the following morning. Patients and parents would camp by the well overnight, and much drunkenness was experienced.

Forfar Several witches were executed here in the seventeenth century. One of the most notorious of them confessed to having eaten babies.

Fortingall Anyone who dropped a penny into the waters of the Iron Well, in Glen Lyon near here, could make a wish with confidence, it used to be believed.

Glamis Glamis Castle, ancestral home of the Bowes-Lyon family, is reputed to be haunted by several ghosts. Strangest of all the stories connected with the castle concerns the so-called 'secret room', the window of which has never been successfully identified from the exterior of the walls. In this room, the family's

'monstrous child' was reputedly hidden. This hideously deformed creature lived for many years, or even centuries. As each heir to the earldom came of age, he was told the dreadful secret and shown the rightful Earl.

Another version of the Glamis legend concerns Alexander, the wicked Earl of Crawford, often referred to as 'Earl Beardie'. Earl Beardie is said to have been playing cards in the castle with a number of his cronies when he was advised to stop, as he was incurring debts that he could not hope to repay. In a fury, Earl Beardie swore that he would play, if he wished, until the Day of Judgment. Immediately, the Devil appeared in the room. Since then, it is believed, Earl Beardie, his friends and the Devil have been gambling together in some secret room in the castle, and will continue to do so until the end of time.

Glen Lyon   In this lonely valley, near the turn into Glen Cailliche, three oddly-shaped stones have been kept in winter time in a small stone dwelling by a stream. Each spring, they have been brought outside and have been left outdoors until the autumn. They are said to represent a man and a woman who once took refuge in the glen, and their daughter, born in this happy and auspicious spot. They are said to bring fair weather and good grazing to the local shepherds.

Lethnot   Many supernatural occurrences have been reported from Lethnot Glen. A water kelpie is said to have haunted a pool beside Craigendownie. A 'White Lady' has been seen walking among trees at the Leuchat. Fairies and a brawny witch have left their marks on the Caterthuns. The Devil is said to have arrived in a cloud of sulphur smoke at Lethnot Mill. One eighteenth-century minister buried a suicide in Lethnot Churchyard. That night, when he was chasing a black cat with a pitchfork, he fell down the manse stairs and broke his neck. The people of Lethnot decided at once that the cat had been the Devil in disguise.

Glamis – ancient castle with many ghosts

Lornty   A ferocious mermaid is said to have been seen by Loch Benachally, out of which flows Lornty Burn.

Schiehallion   This is often called 'The Fairy Hill of Caledonia'. A well on its slopes was believed for centuries to be inhabited by fairies who could grant wishes or cure ailments. It used to be visited with much ceremony on May Day, when girls dressed in white would bring garlands as gifts for the fairies supposed to be living in the well.

Scone   The Palace, here, has associations that go back to the Dark Ages and the Picts. The Abbey Church was the home, for some four hundred years, of the Stone of Destiny, now forming part of the Coronation Chair in Westminster Abbey.

Scotlandwell   The well in the centre of the village is still visited by the sick, who throw coins into its waters. King Robert the Bruce is said to have been cured of leprosy here.

St Fillans   A well a few hundred yards south of the summit of Dundurn, or 'St Fillan's Hill', used to be visited by the sick, most of whom came on 1 May or 1 August. The water was thought to be of special usefulness to barren women.

Struan   The Chiefs of the Struan Robertsons owned, for centuries, a crystal found fortuitously just before the Battle of Bannockburn. As well as being a lucky talisman, it was thought to be capable of curing most illnesses. Patients had to drink water in which the Head of the Clan had dipped the stone three times.

St Vigeans   See **Arbroath**, **Tayside** (above)

Tealing   A well at Baldragon, near here, used to be called 'The Nine Maidens' Well'. According to local tradition, a farmer who had nine pretty daughters sent one of them to this well to fetch some water. When she failed to return, one of her sisters went to look for her. She, too, failed to return. Eight girls, in all, vanished before the ninth and last found the dead bodies of her sisters in the rushes by the well. They were being guarded by a fierce dragon. The dragon seized the ninth maiden, too, but her cries attracted the attention of her lover, a young man called Martin. After a long struggle, Martin managed to slaughter the beast, but his sweetheart did not recover from her injuries.

Trinity-Gask   The water of Holy Trinity Well, near the Manse at Kirkton, was long famous for its cures and as a protection against plague and witchcraft.

Weem Hill   St David's Well, on the side of the hill behind Weem Church, has been regarded from ancient days as a wishing-well worth visiting. Those making wishes would throw pins, buttons and coins into the water.

Further reading
Fraser, Duncan, *Glen of the Rowan Trees*, Standard Press, Montrose, 1974.

Further information from
The Chief Librarian, Central Library, The Wellgate, Dundee, DD1 1DB.
Angus District Libraries and Museums Service, County Buildings, Forfar, DD8 3LG.
Perth and Kinross District Library, Shore Road, Perth, PH2 8BH.

Western Isles

Benbecula, Uist   Women gathering seaweed here, in 1830, are said to have seen a mermaid swimming in the sea. A boy threw stones at the strange creature, and injured her. A few days later, the mermaid's body was washed ashore. The corpse was given a shroud and coffin, and buried on dry land.

Callanish Here, on the Island of Lewis, is a prehistoric stone circle. Avenues of monoliths lead to and from it. The Gaelic name for the stones – 'Fir Chreig', or 'The False Men' – suggests their origin, still thought likely by some local people. The stones, they say, were once giants who lived at Callanish. They would not build a church for themselves, nor would they let themselves be baptised by St Kieran when he came here on a mission. So St Kieran turned them into stone.

Sandray According to J. F. Campbell, author of *Popular Tales of the West Highlands*, published in 1860, a farmer's wife living on Sandray used to lend a kettle every day to a 'woman of peace', or fairy, who lived in a nearby Fairy Hill.

Tarbert The many large boulders near here, on Harris, are said locally to have comprised, once, a giant's castle.

The Shiant The rocky 'Charmed Islands' in the Minch, the channel to the east of Lewis, are constantly battered by powerful waves. These are said in the Outer Hebrides to be stirred up by water kelpies, or 'Blue Men'.

Further reading
Swire, Otta F., *The Outer Hebrides and Their Legends*, Oliver and Boyd, Edinburgh, 1966.

Further information from
The Chief Librarian, Western Isles Libraries, Public Library, Keith Street, Stornoway, Isle of Lewis, PA87 2QG.

The stone circle at Callanish, in the Outer Hebrides

Select Bibliography

Alexander, Marc *Phantom Britain*, Muller, 1975.

Alexander, Marc *Enchanted Britain*, Barker, 1981.

Alexander, Marc *British Folklore, Myths and Legends*, Weidenfeld, 1982.

Ashe, Geoffrey *Avalonian Quest*, Methuen, 1982.

Barber, Chris *Mysterious Wales*, David and Charles, 1982.

Barham, T. *Witchcraft in the Thames Valley*, Spur Books, 1973.

Bord, J. and C. *Sacred Waters*, Granada, 1985.

Bronham, I. J. *Mysteries of Wales*, Celtic Publications, Swansea, 1979.

Brooks, J. A. *Ghosts and Witches of the Cotswolds*, Jarrold, 1981.

Brown, Theo *Ghostly Gold and Goblin Tunes*, Guernsey: Toucan Press, 1969.

Byrne, Tom *Tales from the Past*, Ironmarket Press, 1977.

Dalyell, John Graham *The Darker Superstitions of Scotland*, Griffin, Glasgow, 1835.

Davidson, Thomas *Rowan Tree and Red Thread*, Oliver and Boyd, 1949.

Folklore, Myths and Legends of Britain, The Reader's Digest Association, 1973.

Forman, Joan *Haunted East Anglia*, Hale, 1974.

Forman, Joan *The Haunted South*, Hale, 1978.

Green, Andrew *Our Haunted Kingdom*, Wolfe, 1973.

Green, Andrew *Ghosts of the South East*, David and Charles, 1976.

Grice, Frederick *Folk Tales of the West Midlands*, Thomas Nelson & Sons, 1952.

Hallam, Jack *Ghosts of the North*, David and Charles, 1976.

Henderson, W. *Notes on the Folklore of the Northern Counties of England*, E.P. Publishing, 1973. (Reprint).

Hunt, Robert *Popular Romances of the West of England*, Benjamin Blom, 1968.

Jones, Francis *Holy Wells of Wales*, University of Wales Press, Cardiff, 1954.

Jones, T. Gwyn *Welsh Legends and Folk Tales*, Puffin, 1979.

Legg, Rodney (and others), *Ghosts of Dorset, Devon and Somerset*, Dorset Publishing Co., Milborne Port, 1974.

Lofthouse, Jessica *North-Country Folklore in Lancashire, Cumbria and the Pennine Dales*, Hale, 1976.

Maple, Eric *Supernatural England*, Hale, 1977.

Merril, John *Legends and Folk Lore (The Midlands)*, Wayland, 1974.

Morris, Ruth and Frank *Scottish Healing Wells*, Alethea Press, 1982.

Powell, Roberta Ross *Welsh Tales of the Supernatural*, John Jones, 1979.

Radford, Ken *Tales of South Wales*, Skilton and Shaw, 1979.

Radford, Ken *Tales of North Wales*, Skilton and Shaw, 1982.

Rhys, John *Celtic Folklore, Welsh and Manx*, Oxford University Press, 1901.

Grant Stewart, W. *Popular Superstitions of the Highlands of Scotland*, Ward Lock, 1970 (Reprint).

Swift, Eric *Folk Tales of the East Midlands*, Nelson, 1984.

Sykes, Wirt *British Goblins*, E.P. Publishing, 1973. (Reprint).

Tegner, Henry *Ghosts of the North Country*, Frank Graham, 1974.

Thompson, Francis *The Ghosts, Spirits and Spectres of Scotland*, Impulse, Aberdeen, 1973.

Turner, James *Ghosts in the South-West*, David and Charles, 1973.

Underwood, Peter *The Ghosts of North-West England*, Fontana, 1978.

Underwood, Peter *Ghosts of Wales*, Corgi, 1980.

Watkins, A. *The Old Straight Track*, Methuen, 1948.

West, H. Mills *Ghosts of East Anglia*, Barbara Hopkinson Books, 1984.

Westwood, Jennifer *Albion: A Guide to Legendary Britain*, Granada, 1985.

Whitlock, Ralph *In Search of Lost Gods*, Phaidon, 1979.

Index

Numbers in *italics* refer to illustrations